EEC and the Third World: A Survey 2

Hunger in the World

edited by Christopher Stevens

HOLMES & MEIER PUBLISHERS, INC.
IMPORT DIVISION
IUB Building
30 Irving Place, New York, N.Y. 10003

ISBN 0-8419-0816-8
ISBN 0-8419-0817-6 (pbk.)

First published 1982

Represented in Nigeria by Nigeria Publishers Services Ltd,
P.O. Box 62, Ibadan, Nigeria

Represented in East Africa by K. W. Martin, P.O. Box 30583,
Nairobi, Kenya

Typeset in Monophoto Times by
Macmillan India Ltd., Bangalore
Printed in Great Britain for Hodder and Stoughton Educational,
a division of Hodder and Stoughton Ltd,
Mill Road, Dunton Green, Sevenoaks, Kent,
by Richard Clay (The Chaucer Press) Ltd, Bungay, Suffolk

Contents

Editorial Board

About the Contributors

Robert Cohen is a member of the European Parliament.

Chris Farrands is a Senior Lecturer at Trent Polytechnic, Nottingham.

Adrian Hewitt is a Research Officer at the Overseas Development Institute, London.

Barbara Huddleston is a Research Fellow at the International Food Policy Research Institute, Washington.

Susan Joekes is a Research Officer at the Institute of Development Studies, Sussex.

Fiona Merry was a research student at the University of Sussex during the preparation of this volume, and is currently an economist with Lloyds Bank International, London.

Joan Pearce is a Research Fellow at the Royal Institute of International Affairs, London.

Phil Raikes is a Research Fellow at the Centre for Development Research, Copenhagen.

Geoffrey Shepherd is Deputy Director of the Sussex European Research Centre.

Joan Verloren van Themaat is a Lecturer in economics at the Institute of Social Studies, The Hague.

Ann Weston is a Research Officer at the Overseas Development Institute, London.

Addresses:

Overseas Development Institute,
10–11 Percy Street,
London W1P OJB

The Institute of Development Studies
at the University of Sussex,
Falmer,
Brighton, BN1 9RE

A note on EEC Units of Account

The EEC has used a variety of units to express values. The most commonly used in the context of trade and aid flows are the European Currency Unit (Ecu), established in December 1978 for use in the European Monetary Co-operation Fund, and, until the end of 1980, the European Unit of Account (Eua), which expressed the aid provisions of the Lomé Convention. Both units were based on an identical basket of European currencies but, although the baskets were identical, the two units were not revalued at the same intervals and so at any one time they might have slightly different values in terms of other currencies. Since January 1981, all aid and trade values have been expressed in terms of Ecu alone. The Ecu comprises the sum of the following amounts, and its value in relation to other currencies is given in the statistical appendix.

German mark	0.828
Pound sterling	0.0885
French franc	1.15
Italian lira	109
Dutch guilder	0.286
Belgian franc	3.66
Luxembourg franc	0.14
Danish krone	0.217
Irish pound	0.00759

List of Abbreviations

ACP	African, Caribbean and Pacific (signatories to the Lomé Conventions)
AEC	Assistance Evaluation Committee (of the Wheat Council)
CAP	Common Agricultural Policy
CFA	FAO Committee on Food Aid Programmes and Policies
CFF	Compensatory Financing Facility (of the IMF)
DAC	Development Assistance Committee
dcs	developed countries
DG	Directorate General (of the EEC Commission)
EDF	European Development Fund
EEC	European Economic Community
EFTA	European Free Trade Area
EIB	European Investment Bank
FAC	Food Aid Convention
FAO	Food and Agriculture Organisation of the United Nations
FSAS	Food Security Assistance Scheme (of FAO)
GATT	General Agreement on Tariffs and Trade
GSP	Generalised System of Preferences
IDA	International Development Association
IEFR	International Emergency Food Reserve
IMF	International Monetary Fund
IWA	International Wheat Agreement
ldcs	developing countries
lldcs	least developed countries
MFA	Multifibre Arrangement
mfn	most favoured nation
NICs	Newly Industrialising Countries
NTB	Non-tariff import barrier
SADCC	Southern African Development Co-ordination Conference
SNAP	Substantial New Action Programme
VER	Voluntary Export Restraint
WFC	World Food Council
WFP	World Food Programme

Editorial Policy

The Survey provides an annual record of and commentary on major developments in the European Community's economic relations with the Third World. Its audience includes policy makers, opinion formers and academics in the ten member countries and the Commission, and in North America and the Third World. Its underlying philosophy is that the EEC and the Third World have mutual interests. Neither harmony nor conflict of such interests is regarded as inevitable.

The Editorial Board is responsible for determining that this work should be presented to the public, but individual members of the Board are not responsible for statements of fact and expressions of opinion contained therein.

Foreword

This is the second of an annual series of *Surveys* which will review and comment upon major developments in the EEC's economic relations with the Third World. Like the first issue, it aims to fill a major gap by pulling together the many strands of EEC (and, where relevant, member state) policies and actions that affect the Third World, and to bring to this assessment the weight of research being undertaken in European centres and elsewhere. It is, of course, highly selective; the aim is not to produce a voluminous yearbook of events, but to survey the state of EEC-Third World relations at a regular interval, focussing on key trends and events, as identified by the Board. This *Survey* retains the same pattern of authorship as its predecessor in order to produce a well-rounded commentary and record. It also retains statistical and documentary appendices, and adds to these a select bibliographical appendix containing books and articles recently published in the EEC which, in the view of the Editorial Board, provide valuable information and analyses on EEC-Third World relations.

The extensive research and editorial work required for the *Survey* continues to receive generous financial support from the Institute of Development Studies, the Noel Buxton Trust and the Shell Grants Committee; in addition, the Centre for Development Research, Copenhagen, with financial support from the Danish International Development Agency (DANIDA) and the EEC, very kindly hosted a workshop in June 1981 at which the contributors to this *Survey* presented papers.

London
September 1981

1

Hunger in the World: Does the EEC Exacerbate It or Alleviate It?

This second survey of relationships between the EEC and the Third World takes its sub-title and its theme from the European Parliament's report on 'Hunger in the World'. Like the Parliament, it recognises that the causes of hunger are not to be found solely in the realm of agricultural policy, still less in the agricultural policies of the developing countries themselves, though these are important. In a feature at the end of this introductory chapter, the Dutch Euro-MP, Robert Cohen, explains why the Parliament devoted the energies of five committees for a year to this issue, and what response this effort has provoked. He emphasises the wide-ranging nature of the enquiry, which is summed up in the opening lines of the Parliament's resolution. This asserts that the alleviation of hunger in developing countries (ldcs) requires 'a substantial improvement in the purchasing power of their peoples' and that this will involve 'far-reaching adjustments to the production methods and way of life in the industrialised countries.'[1] Hunger in ldcs is an aspect of poverty. Therefore, policies that reduce poverty have the potential to alleviate hunger, and conversely those that increase poverty can exacerbate hunger. Increasing wealth is not a sufficient condition for reducing hunger, but it is a necessary condition.

The EEC's position on the Multifibre Arrangement (MFA), the Generalised System of Preferences (GSP) and reform of the Common Agricultural Policy (CAP) are therefore just as relevant to the question posed in the title of this chapter as are its policies on international food security, aid to agriculture and the special needs of the least developed countries. Indeed, the question only makes complete sense in relation to this wide range of influences. If the question of world hunger is considered solely within the ambit of 'development aid policy' narrowly defined, it is difficult to argue that the EEC seriously exacerbates the problem; the worst that could be said is that its efforts are ineffective or inefficient. But if it is acknowledged that hunger in the ldcs is also affected by a host of other EEC policies and actions, many of which are framed without any direct reference to the ldcs, then the question becomes very apposite. During 1980/81 the EEC Commission tended to acknowledge this wider link, while the Council of Ministers tended to ignore it.

The Commission supports a global initiative

For a variety of reasons, including the influence of bureaucratic imperatives and personalities, the EEC Commission has tended to be a strong force for a sympathetic and wide-ranging policy towards the Third World. Within the Commission the directorate-general for development (DG8) is larger and more influential in relation to other directorates-general than are many of the development departments of the member states. This influence is due partly to the fact that it actually has a programme to implement (unlike some directorates-general) and to the personality of its long-serving Commissioner, Claude Cheysson, who left office in 1981 to become the new socialist Foreign Minister of France. DG8's role is rooted in the administration of the Community's aid programme, but it has been able to spread its influence into areas of North-South relations that, in many of the member states, are the preserve of the foreign ministry. Nonetheless, it is not alone in formulating Commission proposals on issues relevant to the Third World. It shares responsibility for ldcs outside the charmed circle of African, Caribbean and Pacific (ACP) signatories of the Lomé Conventions with the directorate-general for external relations (DG1) which has also played a leading role in North-South trade negotiations, notably the GSP and MFA. Moreover, the directorate-general for agriculture (DG6) has clear precedence on issues that fall within the ambit of the CAP.

The Commission's position in 1981 was encapsulated in proposals it sent to the Council of Ministers in March 1981. The proposals were drafted as a basis for the Community's strategy at the Western economic summit in Ottawa in July, and the Cancun summit scheduled for October 1981. The report was tabled at the Maastricht Council meeting of 22–24 March which referred it to a North-South working group of the COREPER which, in turn, reported to the Luxembourg Council meeting of 29–30 June. A comparison of the document adopted by the Council in June 1981 and the proposals of the Commission (particularly as elaborated in an extensive communication to Council in May 1981[2]) well illustrates the differences in approach between these two key bodies.

The Commission's position is that the current economic problems of the industrialised countries must be solved within the context of North-South relations. It emphasises three aspects of this relationship between the North's economic problems and its relations with the South. The first concerns restructuring of production in the industrialised countries. While this is not primarily a North-South issue, it does have aspects that affect the Third World, notably the need for the industrialised countries to accommodate imports of manufactured goods from the newly industrialising countries (NICs), and to increase exports to the Third World. The second aspect concerns the emergence of scarcities, particularly in energy and food. Finally, the Commission stresses what it calls the 'geopolitical dimension to the crisis' of the industrialised countries and the necessity for the EEC of 'maintaining stability in its neighbouring regions' by such devices as the Euro-Arab dialogue and the Lomé Conventions. These considerations led the Commission to propose three guidelines for Community policy:

(i) the scarcity constraints that weigh heavily on the world economy should be eased, particularly those relating to energy and food;
(ii) development financing should be improved in such a way as to prevent a worsening of the economic situation of the developing countries and, as a consequence, to improve economic activity in the industrialised countries;
(iii) policies should be adopted which would enable the Community to pursue its efforts to restructure its manufacturing base while ensuring greater access for developing country products and hence make the Community better able to withstand competition from the major industrialised countries.[3]

This reference to competition from other industrialised countries highlights one of the major themes of the Commission's report, which is to contrast EEC interests and policies with those of the USA. 'Of the industrialised countries', it argues, 'Europe is probably the one with the biggest immediate economic interest in reduction of constraints caused by scarcities and of unstable modes of behaviour.'[4] The United States, by contrast, is more preoccupied with domestic economic balances and bilateral aid. The EEC should, therefore, take the initiative and 'emphasise to its partners, particularly the United States and Japan, the link between, on the one hand, the economic and political security of Europe, and by extension of the whole of the Western world, and, on the other hand, the re-establishment of international economic relations offering sufficiently attractive prospects to its developing partners'.

A second major theme of the report is that the South is affected by a wide range of EEC policies, not just those traditionally associated with development aid. On energy it recognises the need for both increased investment in Third World energy production (and the creation of an energy affiliate of the World Bank) and greater energy saving in the industrialised countries. On food, it proposes both increased aid to agriculture and greater access to the EEC market for imports of agricultural products. On trade, it sees the need both for investment protection in ldcs and for an open EEC market for manufactured and processed commodity imports.

The report produced by the Council's North-South committee and tabled at its Luxembourg summit is a much shorter document, which excludes the main issues of contention between the Ten, which were put on one side. In general, the report adopts a similar line to that of the Commission on its first major theme, the need for an EEC initiative, while being more reticent on the second, particularly where it involves EEC imports from the ldcs. In particular, the Council adopted three policies for the Ottawa and Cancun summits which were expected to bring it into conflict with the USA:

– the prompt resumption of the UN 'Global Negotiations', which have been stalled since the failure of the Eleventh Special Session of the General Assembly in August/September 1980 to agree to an agenda (when USA, Britain and Germany took particularly hardline positions);

– qualified support for a World Bank energy affiliate; the qualification being that the EEC does not rule out a different institutional arrangement provided that the alternative retains two key features of the proposed affiliate which are that it mobilises additional public resources as well as private resources, and that it has an institutional link with the OPEC countries;

– support for an increase in the resources of the international financial institutions by doubling the capital of the World Bank, proceeding with the sixth replenishment of its soft-loan window, the IDA, and increasing the intervention capability of the IMF.

This tone of concern with USA policies on North-South was mirrored by a similar concern on the part of EEC leaders attending Ottawa about other aspects of USA policy. It was expected, therefore, that the summit would be dominated by disagreement between the US president and the rest. A typical press comment before the summit was the *Financial Times* headline, 'Educating Mr. Reagan'.[5] In the event, the communiqué implied that there had been a meeting of minds, not least on North-South issues which featured quite prominently (although not nearly as prominently as had been expected immediately after the Venice Western economic summit of 1980). The section of the communiqué dealing with North-South issues is reproduced in the Documentary Appendix. It indicated progress on all three of the North-South positions that had been expected to bring the EEC into conflict with the USA. It expressed support for a resumption of the Global Negotiations, for providing the international financial institutions with the resources they need, and for increased finance for ldc energy development with a commitment 'to explore . . . possible mechanisms, such as those being examined in the World Bank . . .'

Immediate reaction to the Ottawa summit was therefore positive. However, it remains to be seen how far these necessarily brief references to complex issues mask differences of approach. Despite the favourable noises made in the Ottawa communiqué the USA delegation to the UN conference on new and renewable sources of energy, held in Nairobi a month later, stalled proposals to support the proposed World Bank energy affiliate. Clashes between the EEC and the USA may continue, therefore, into 1982. Indeed, the change of government in France appears to have increased the likelihood that there will continue to be major differences of approach to Third World issues.

Globalism versus regionalism

EEC global initiatives on North-South relations stand in a sometimes uneasy relationship with its regionally-oriented aid and preferential trade policy. The Lomé Convention still forms the core of DG8's activity, and the Commission is planning to begin preparations in 1982 for negotiating a successor to Lomé II. However, the Lomé Convention received a number of rude knocks during 1980/81. By far the largest was the failure of Stabex to meet its commitments. The Stabex system was conceived as an insurance scheme that would cover the ACP against cyclical falls in their export earnings. Its main *raison d'etre* was removed before it ever came into operation under Lomé I, because in 1975 the IMF extended the size and scope of its much larger compensatory financing facility which has similar aims, and because during the Lomé negotiations one of the unique features of Stabex, which would have channelled payments to the afflicted commodities, was dropped. Nonetheless, the scheme has proved to be very popular with the ACP for a variety of reasons (see *Survey 1*, Chapter 3).

The finance available for Stabex is drawn from the quinquennial European Development Fund (EDF) agreed under each Lomé Convention. The global amount for the quinquennium is fixed, but there is scope for carrying over or bringing forward a certain proportion of funds from one year's tranche to another. Claims on Stabex are based on the world market prices of the commodities included in the scheme over the preceding four years. Because cocoa and coffee prices fell sharply in the late 1970s, there has been a sharp increase in claims on Stabex, exacerbated in 1980 by a poor groundnut harvest. As a result, Stabex ran out of cash in 1981. Claims arising from 1980 totalled some 260 million ecus while the finance available (including unspent monies carried over from Lomé I and the maximum drawdown from the 1981 tranche) totalled only 138 million ecus. As a result, Stabex claims have had to be cut by about half, although the EEC and ACP agreed on a differential formula for cuts favouring the least developed. The transfers approved in 1981 in respect of 1980 are given in the Statistical Appendix. Since the underlying causes of the high claims will continue in 1981, it is likely that next year there will be a similar problem.

The problems of 1981 have a significance not only for Stabex but also for the ACP group. The fact that Stabex's financial basis is unequal to its stated goal has been pointed out on several occasions (not least in *Survey 1*). Hence, a cash crisis was predictable. Of possibly greater long-term significance was the reaction of the ACP to this shortfall. At the EEC-ACP Council of Ministers summit in Luxembourg in April 1981 the ACP agreed to the cuts, but at the time the precise scale of the shortfall was not known and many of the ACP ministers apparently believed that the cuts would be quite small – around 25 %. When the true picture emerged at a meeting of the joint committee of ambassadors on 19 June there were howls of protest. The president of the ACP council of ministers, Hugh Shearer of Jamaica, wrote to the EEC council president, Lord Carrington, in July to request an emergencey ministerial summit to discuss both Stabex and the EEC's decision to offer the ACP sugar exporters a lower price increase than that accorded to beet producers (see Chapter 2). Although the precise scale of the Stabex shortfall was unknown at the time of the April meeting in Luxembourg, a rough guide could have been obtained quite easily by studying recent price trends. The fact that the ACP ministers did not have this information illustrates a more general problem that they tend not to be well-organised and briefed in negotiations with the EEC. This is partly because the ministers have tended to curb the scope for initiative of the ACP secretariat which was created to provide a group civil service.

Other jolts to the Lomé Convention in 1980/81 occurred in relation to Greece and to Southern Africa. As explained in *Survey 1* (Chapter 4), the ldcs may suffer as a result of enlargement of the EEC, particularly when Spain joins. The ACP have no major problems with Greek accession, but they were anxious to establish a precedent of full consultation by the EEC to safeguard their interests against the day when Spain joins. In the event, the arrangements for Greek entry were negotiated entirely between Greece and the Nine, without direct reference to the ACP even over the transitional regime covering Greece's implementation of the Lomé Convention. Instead, the EEC and ACP signed a joint declaration (reproduced in the Documentary Appendix) which notes that enlargement 'can be a cause of concern to the ACP states', but promises only that in relation to Spanish and Portuguese membership the EEC will 'keep the ACP states appropriately informed'.

In Southern Africa, the year began well with Zimbabwe signing the Lomé Convention on 4 November 1980. Although ratification of the accession treaty by the parliaments of Zimbabwe and the Ten was unlikely to be completed before the end of 1981, there seemed no doubt that the country would become the 60th ACP state. When it is ratified, Zimbabwe will be entitled to an aid allocation of some 85 million ecu under the EDF, and in the interim it is receiving 14.5 million ecus of aid from the non-associate budget. Similarly, a transitional trade regime came into effect on 1 January 1981 providing identical treatment to that accorded under the Lomé Convention.

The problems in Southern Africa have arisen in relation to Angola and Mozambique. Neither country has so far been willing to sign the Lomé Convention despite hopes in the Commission that Zimbabwe's membership would pave the way. There are several reasons for their reluctance not all of which are entirely clear. However, it is believed in the

Community that East German pressure has been influential, particularly in the case of Mozambique, and the whole issue has been sucked into the dispute between the two Germanies. While not willing to sign Lomé, the two countries have expressed an interest in obtaining EEC aid from the non-associates budget. However, there has been some opposition to this in the Council of Ministers. The West Germans, in particular, have opposed aid and, despite strong support for Angola and Mozambique from Holland, Denmark, Ireland and Italy, a substantial amount of the non-associate aid earmarked for these two states has been transferred to Zimbabwe. The issue is likely to come to a head before the end of 1981. This is because the regional aid vote for Southern Africa under Lomé II is likely to be committed to projects that are related to schemes in Angola and Mozambique, since both countries are members of SADCC. Some 60 % of the regional vote is allocated to transport, and the current chairman of the SADCC transport commission is the Mozambique minister of transport.

Outside of the Lomé framework, there have been a number of positive developments in the field of conventional aid. The most significant is the adoption of a formal procedure for approving non-associate aid. Unlike the EDF, allocations to the non-associate programme are decided annually and are drawn from the Community budget. Since the programme began in 1976, the system for allocating aid between countries and projects has been governed by an ad hoc procedure. Under this, the Commission has proposed annually to the Council a brief description of the entire year's programme. The proposal has had to run the gamut of all the tiers of committees that separate the Commission and the Council, so that the Council has not normally given its approval until around October/November of each year. In 1981 a permanent procedure was at last approved. Under it there will be a committee of member state representatives (analogous to the EDF committee) which will meet regularly to consider Commission proposals for support to particular projects and which can take a decision by a qualified majority. The size of the non-associate programme is shown in the Statistical Appendix. It is small by comparison with the EDF, but it has grown rapidly since its inception and reached 150 million ecu in 1981. Moreover, it is disbursed more rapidly than the EDF, partly because most of the money is used on projects that are co-financed with other donors that undertake the bulk of the necessary project appraisal. As a result of this speed, one-third of the EEC's actual disbursements of official development assistance in 1979 were to non-Lomé (i.e. associate and non-associate) states, and this proportion is expected to be higher in 1980.

Hunger in the World

The extent to which the EEC adopts a 'global' policy towards the Third World is important in two senses for its contribution to the alleviation of hunger in the world. In the geographical sense, the regional focus for aid and trade preferences inevitably leads to a relative neglect of poverty in countries outside the charmed circle. As Joan Verloren van Themaat makes clear in Chapter 8, the EEC is a major influence on the economies of the least developed countries. But, as Adrian Hewitt demonstrates in Chapter 9, EEC policy towards the least developed is weakened by ambiguities that stem from its regional approach. The problems of the least developed have been highlighted because they are particularly ill-placed to benefit from the world trading system and require special assistance. Adrian Hewitt examines the nature of the special treatment they currently receive from the EEC, while Joan Verloren van Themaat questions the relevance of conventional prescriptions such as those being tabled at the UN conference on the least developed scheduled to convene in Paris just as this *Survey* went to press.

The other sense in which globalism is important is the EEC's perception of the breadth of North-South issues. The other chapters of this *Survey* take a broad view of the causes of hunger. In this they are in accord with the position of the European Parliament and the Commission, at least in some of its statements. But the Council of Ministers has tended to take a more narrowly defined position reflecting the perceptions of some member states. Chapters 2–7 of this *Survey* relate to the EEC as a major producing and trading region, and show how its domestic agricultural and industrial policies, as well as its trade regime can affect the Third World, for good or ill, to a much greater extent than does its aid policy. At a time of rising protectionist pressure, the Community has successfully resisted many attempts to restrict imports from the developing countries. Yet it is difficult not to agree with Chris Farrands (Chapter 6) in relation to the MFA that 'while no one in the EEC has any intention of harming the developing countries as a deliberate action, the net effect . . . is to produce a policy which has profound and generally harmful effects on ldc producers', or with the comment of Geoffrey Shepherd (Chapter 4) that 'protectionism has a capacity for spreading, however specifically it is intended to apply'.

Notes

1 European Parliament Working Documents 1980–81. Document 1-341/80, 29 August 1980.
2 *Community Policy for the North-South Dialogue*, COM(81) 68 final, 7 May 1981.
3 COM(81) 68 final, p. 9.
4 Ibid. p. 7.
5 *Financial Times* 17 July 1981.

Feature: The European Parliament and Hunger in the World

Robert Cohen MEP

The initial interest in world hunger

In September 1979, very shortly after its first meeting, the new directly elected European Parliament turned its attention to four different proposals concerning the problem of hunger in the world. One of the draft resolutions was tabled by Mr Pannella; the others came from the Socialist Group, the Italian Communists, and the European People's Party, as the Christian Democrats call themselves in the European Parliament. Following the customary procedure these draft resolutions were not discussed directly in the plenary assembly, but were passed on to the relevant committee for more detailed study – in this case the Committee on Development and Cooperation.

The fact that the new Parliament wished to concern itself intensively with the problem of developing countries so soon after its inauguration is not surprising in itself. It is true that in the election campaign the emphasis was placed primarily on internal European problems, such as the fight against unemployment, energy policy, democratisation of the decision-making process, etc.; but nonetheless many representatives wanted to make it clear that the direct elections were not just an intra-European affair but that Europe should also look at what was happening outside and was alive to the needs of the Third World. Hunger and malnutrition are undoubtedly the worst scourges afflicting many people in developing countries; without food one cannot even begin to think about further economic and social development. On the other hand, of course, hunger is not an isolated phenomenon and it cannot be divorced from the other factors and circumstances which determine the fate of many developing countries. Hunger is an economic problem not merely a physical one, and is rooted primarily in a lack of purchasing power and, in some cases, non-existent communications.

Given these underlying causes, the European Parliament might conceivably have taken a completely different approach, for instance one more directly aimed at creating better opportunities for development by means of a specific Community trade policy or increased financial assistance. Such an approach would undoubtedly have been more professional, but less spectacular. That the more spectacular approach was chosen was a direct result of the initiative taken by Mr Pannella, who was the first to come up with a proposal for a resolution. Pannella, a member of the Italian Radical Party belonging to the small group of MEPs who have come together to form the 'Technical Coordination Group', was already a well-known figure on the Italian political scene because of his antics and unconventional behaviour. On his home ground his activities were indeed sometimes successful but results were more difficult to achieve in the European context. To begin with, Pannella went in for radical pronouncements, whether they seemed likely to bear fruit or not, but the representatives of the other groups chose a more substantial course of action. The Committee on Development and Cooperation studied the four draft resolutions at its October meeting and instructed the authors to come up with a common text. At that stage of the proceedings Pannella as good as withdrew, not being interested in watered-down compromises. A common text was worked out and discussed by Parliament that same month at a plenary. However, Pannella had again tabled dozens of amendments and, to prevent the deliberations from dragging on for hours, the resolution was referred back to the Committee at the request of the Chairman of the Committee on Development and Cooperation.

At a meeting of the Committee held in November it was provisionally agreed to leave out all the amendments and a draft resolution was approved which later the same month was also passed by Parliament itself. In this resolution the Committee on Development and Cooperation was instructed 'to draw up by February 1980 a comprehensive and fundamental report on how the European Community could and should make a practical contribution towards eliminating world hunger'.

The detailed report

The Committee on Development and Cooperation had already at its November meeting approved a proposal drawn up by the Socialist members on the Committee regarding the procedure for producing a report on 'Hunger in the World'. The Socialist porposal was aimed at involving all the major groups in the operation right from the beginning so that at the final stage of the proceedings it would be difficult for them to shirk their responsibility. Normally a report in the European Parliament is drawn up by one person designated by one of the groups after joint consideration of the matter. In the case of 'Hunger in the World' the Italian Communist, Bruno Ferrero, was appointed overall rapporteur, but at the same time a working party was set up, in accordance with a proposal from the Socialists, consisting of five sub-rapporteurs. These sub-rapporteurs were each to take one aspect of the very wide subject so that their reports could form a basis for a final resolution to be drawn up by Ferrero for Parliament's approval. The five sub-rapporteurs were all of different nationalities and came from different groups. They were Mrs Focke (German Social Democrat), Mr Pannella (Italian Radical), Mr Sablé (French Liberal), Mr Simmonds (UK Conservative) and Mr Vergeer (Dutch Christian Democrat). They were given the task of writing sub-reports on such diverse subjects as: food aid policy and emergency aid; coordination of development policies of the Member States and the Community; the relationship between agricultural production and food aid policy; international trade and organization of the major markets in basic foodstuffs; financial and technical cooperation for the development of agricultural production. At the same time it was decided that while the Committee on Development and Cooperation would have principal responsibility for the subject, a number of other Committees would make recommendations to it. These were the Committees on Political Affairs, Agriculture, External Economic Relations, the Environment, Public Health and Consumer Protection. They also appointed rapporteurs: a UK Conservative, a Danish Liberal, a German Social Democrat and an Italian Communist.

So, right from the beginning, a large number of committees, nearly all the political groups and most nationalities were involved in the exercise. And it was also clear right from the start that the February 1980 deadline could not be kept. While it would have been difficult to make the deadline even with the normal procedure, involving one overall rapporteur, the approach chosen made this a complete non-starter. The European Parliament's usual organizational problems – finding the right place and time for meetings and, even more important, the problems of translation – played an even bigger role than was normally the case. In the event the resolution had to wait until the September 1980 plenary. Prior to that meeting public hearings were also organized in order not to rely exclusively on the expertise and knowledge available within the European Parliament and the European Community but to consult such organizations as FAO and the World Food Council. The organization of these hearings was immediately agreed to by Parliament's Bureau and the hearings were arranged for 18–19 February 1980,[1] and 1–2 April 1980.[2] The sub-rapporteurs had completed their reports in the meantime – with the exception of Pannella, who did not make the effort – and on the basis of these additional reports, the hearings, and other contacts Ferrero drew up his resolution. It was approved in July 1980 by the Committee on Development and Cooperation and was adopted almost unanimously by Parliament's September 1980 plenary.

Response to the report

It is hardly surprising that this resolution, having been so carefully prepared, contains more than mere pronouncements on the problem of hunger as such.[3] It touches upon the North-South Dialogue and the Brandt Report, agricultural development in developing countries and food aid, the Community's agricultural policy and access to the EEC for agricultural products, international trade and financial aid, the Common Fund and international commodity agreements. It is now, however, almost a year since the resolution was adopted and it is justifiable to ask what results all these efforts have now yielded. It is a question which is easier to ask than to answer. First of all it must of course be borne in mind that the European Parliament – despite its name – is not a real parliament. It has no legislative powers, and consequently the adoption of a resolution does not mean that all the points made in it will be converted into law. Even if Parliament did have such powers, however, the hunger problem could not be solved in a year, or even in five years. The resolution is regarded by the European Commission as an important basic statement, which it hopes to use as a starting point for future action. At every meeting of the Committee on Development and Cooperation since the adoption of the resolution, Commission representatives have reported on the progress or lack of progress made. The members of the Committee on Development and Cooperation are putting great pressure on the Commission representatives and using the resolution as a kind of bible with not just ten but scores of commandments. This seems for the present to be the only way: constantly to hammer home that the right amount and the right kind of food aid must be granted, that the Community should open up its frontiers to exports from developing countries, that the Community should play an active role in the North-South Dialogue, and that more budget funds should be made available for development aid.

The Ferrero resolution acts as a prop for all these efforts, especially as it was adopted almost unanimously. The initiators of the move succeeded in their undertaking, and the unusual method used by Parliament to draw up the resolution did not fall short of its objective. All the parties concerned appeared so committed to the work that it was difficult to distance oneself from the results afterwards. Admittedly, hunger is a subject which lends itself to such an approach, but there are probably many other subjects which justify taking a similar tack. In any event the result prompted the Lomé countries to request in the Convention's Consultative Assembly that a working party be set up to study the problem of hunger, with the main focus on the problems in the Lomé countries. This working party has now been set up and is made up of members of the European Parliament and elected representatives from the Lomé countries. It is making rapid progress and will probably manage to produce a report before the end of 1981.

There is another area in which the European Parliament is showing an active interest in Third World problems. Although the Council of Ministers did not deem it necessary to consult Parliament about the Commission Communication on the UNCTAD Conference on the least developed countries held in Paris in September, Parliament itself took the initiative of producing a report and formulating a resolution on it. This resolution too was adopted almost unanimously. It can be seen from these examples that the European Parliament is aware of its responsibilities towards the developing countries. It is clear that Parliament alone cannot solve these countries' problems – something more is called for. But the situation would be worse if the European Parliament ceased to show any interest in these problems on the grounds that it has no powers. This, then, is what has been achieved over the last two years, and it is only to be hoped that events over the next three years of Parliament's term will not cause these efforts to have been in vain.

Notes

1 The participants included Mr Tanco, President of the World Food Council and Minister for Agriculture of the Philippines; Mr Brandt, Chairman of Germany's Social Democratic Party and President of the North-South Commission; Mr Gilman, member of the United States Presidential Committee on World Hunger; Mr Diouf, Minister of Scientific and Technical Research of Senegal; Mr Huda, Minister of Finance of Bangladesh; and Mr Chonchol, former Minister of Agriculture of Chile.

2 Participants included Mr Saouma, Director-General of the FAO; Mr Parotte, Executive Secretary of the International Wheat Council; Mr Shihata, Secretary-General of the OPEC Special Fund; Mr van Gennip, representing Caritas Internationalis; Mr Jackson, representing OXFAM; Mr Thomas, a member of the Board of Unilever; Mr Doumeng, from the Compagnie Interagra; Mr de Maeyer, from the World Health Organization; Professor Mazoyer from the Institut National Agronomique in Paris; and Professor Lipton from the Institute of Development Studies, University of Sussex.

3 Report drawn up on behalf of the Committee on Development and Cooperation on the European Community's contribution to the campaign against hunger in the world. (29.8.1980 – Rapporteur: Mr B Ferrero – Document 1-341/80.)

Part 1

Agricultural Protectionism and the Third World

2

The EEC and Third World Food and Agriculture

Barbara Huddleston, Fiona Merry, Phil Raikes and Christopher Stevens

As Robert Cohen makes clear in the feature at the end of Chapter 1, hunger is an economic problem rooted in a lack of purchasing power. Its alleviation, therefore, can involve action in areas that, at first sight, have little to do with food or agriculture. It is for this reason that both the European Parliament's report on *Hunger in the World* and this *Survey* cover industrial trade and financial flows as well as agricultural production and trade. However, despite the fact that the Generalised System of Preferences or the Multi-Fibre Arrangement can have at least as great an impact on hunger as can food aid, it is convenient to begin the detailed chapters of this *Survey* with an analysis of EEC policies in the realm of agriculture and food. This chapter examines EEC policies that are directly (although not exclusively) related to developing countries, while the next chapter examines the common agricultural policy which forms the foundation on which all other agricultural policies are based: if the foundation shifts, how will this affect the policies that are linked directly to ldcs?

This chapter begins with an outline of the EEC's stated policy on food and agriculture as it affects the ldcs. It moves on to examine EEC policy on the world food trade in the light of an analysis of the needs of food importing ldcs in respect of world food security. It then shifts attention to EEC policies that directly affect food production in ldcs: its aid to agricultural projects in Third World states; and its import regime in respect of ldc agricultural exports, with a focus on sugar.

EEC policy on food and agriculture

The Commission's communication to the Council of Ministers on the North-South Dialogue in May 1981, the role of which is explained in

Chapter 1, contains specific policy recommendations on Third World food and agriculture.[1] It claims that the shortage of food is 'the main scarcity constraint at world level', although the document as a whole tends to give greater weight to energy and financial flows. Its analysis reveals a fine balance between the advocates of greater agricultural production in the EEC as a solution to the scarcity constraint and the view that the alleviation of food shortages in the Third World can only be achieved satisfactorily by increasing production in the ldcs themselves. Thus, while it refers to 'the effort required of all the exporting countries to step up supply' it also makes clear that they 'can step up their supply only by incurring higher production costs since increased output requires large quantities of energy and there are increasingly serious difficulties in trade because of storage and transport problems'. The Commission's proposed remedies fall into three categories:

- measures to increase food production in the ldcs. The international community 'in particular the EEC' should provide support for ldc food strategies, allocate increasing quantities of financial aid to food and agricultural development schemes, and assist relevant research activities.
- measures to improve the operations of the international food trade on which food deficit ldcs will continue to rely, in the medium-term at least. The EEC is urged to assist efforts to make world markets for food products more stable, to establish its own export policy in view of the fact that it 'does not possess adequate machinery to provide greater security of supplies to the developing countries and permit easier access to such supplies', and to improve access to the EEC market for ldc agricultural exports.
- measures to assist weak countries faced with unexpected food shortfalls by increasing the quantity and quality of food aid, and by supporting measures such as the IMF food financing facility to enable afflicted countries to purchase food on the world market.

This chapter addresses all three areas, and seeks to identify the kind of action that is required and the extent to which the EEC's practice measures up to the policy proposals of the Commission. However, as explained in Chapter 1, the Commission's proposals are not the same as EEC policy; they are merely one step in the formulation of policy. The Commission's communication was referred by the Council to a high level committee on North-South which, in turn, reported to the June 1981 meeting of the Council in Luxembourg which adopted the committee's report. This report is much shorter than the Commission's communication, partly because the North-South committee put on one side all the proposals on which there were significant differences of opinion. A comparison of the two documents indicates, therefore, the areas of controversy, although it does not reveal their depth. Like the Commission document, the report adopted by the Council recognises that a solution to the ldcs' food problems lies primarily in increasing food production in the developing countries themselves, and that the EEC should assist this by devoting an increasing proportion of its aid to projects that promote agricultural production directly or do so indirectly (for example by providing necessary infrastructure) and by improving the implementation of the aid. It also recognises that many ldcs will remain dependent upon imports for some time and therefore supports measures to increase security and predictability. In particular, it argues that a new international wheat agreement is essential, that there should be aid in kind and in cash to build up food stocks in the ldcs, and that the volume and modalities of food aid should be adjusted to enable the international community to respond to emergencies, to assist those ldcs with structural food deficits and, through combination with other forms of aid, to assist agricultural development projects. However, it is silent on several topics raised by the Commission: the desirability in this context of increasing EEC production, of an export policy and of improved access to EEC markets for ldc exports. In other words, it is focussed much more narrowly on traditional measures that see the problem as primarily concerning the ldcs, rather than being equally the creation of the rich countries, and its solution as involving the rich countries in helping the ldcs to solve their problems, rather than in altering their own practices. This is not the viewpoint of this *Survey*. However, since the Council has taken this stance, it is desirable to begin with an examination of its policies that are related directly to the needs of food deficit ldcs: world food trade security, and aid to food production.

World food security

Since 1974 the international community, including the EEC, has repeatedly pronounced in favour of creating a world food security system so that a repetition of the acute supply shortfall of the early 1970s could be avoided. After seven years these pronouncements have crystallised into rhetorical support for and some forward movement on a concrete set of policy measures which, if implemented together, would constitute such a system. The key elements relate to three important areas in which it is thought the international community could and should take collective action: food reserves, food aid, and food trade. The most recent formulation of the proposed measures is contained in documentation prepared for the seventh ministerial session of the World Food Council (WFC) in the spring of 1981.[2] The Council's Executive Director suggests eight measures which, taken together, would provide an adequate net for world food security:

- conclusion of a new Wheat Trade Convention;
- accelerated construction of food infrastructure in developing countries;

- establishment of an International Monetary Fund (IMF) food facility;
- renewal of the Food Aid Convention (FAC) for five years at a 10 million ton level;
- annual replenishment of the International Emergency Food Reserve (IEFR) at 500,000 tons and a review of its nature and reliability;
- strengthening the World Food Programme (WFP);
- agreement on a set of food crisis contingency measures;
- establishment of a food crisis contingency reserve.

Of these eight, one has already been achieved, five could reasonably be covered by the new approach to an International Wheat Agreement currently under consideration by the International Wheat Council, and the other two are under active consideration by the FAO Committee on Food Aid Programmes and Policies (CFA). In all except the second, the EEC plays an important role in the relevant decision-making bodies.

IMF food facility

The measure on which progress has already been achieved is the IMF food facility. Acting in response to a suggestion by the FAO and the WFC, the executive board of the IMF began considering the creation of a special facility to finance excess cereal import costs of developing country members in early 1980. After two detailed discussions, and expressions of support from a number of national and international bodies, including the Brandt Commission and the European Parliament, the IMF board decided in May 1981 to provide such assistance by broadening the terms of reference of the existing compensatory financing facility (CFF). Previously, the CFF permitted countries to draw from the Fund if they faced balance of payments problems because their *actual* export earnings in a given year fell short of the *expected* value. Now, the calculation will take into account cost overruns for cereal imports as well as shortfalls in export earnings. Either factor alone or both together can qualify a country for assistance. However, if one offsets the other, assistance is reduced by that amount.

The food facility is primarily a financing mechanism which seeks to assure countries that they do not have to use their own foreign exchange reserves to finance sudden, unexpected increases in the cost of cereal imports which may arise either because of shortfalls in their own harvests or because of sharp increases in prices on the world grain market. Despite the fact that countries have to repay what they draw over a three-year period, beginning three years after the year in which compensation was received, and to pay interest on their drawings, although at subsidised rates, the facility affords a breathing space during which it is hoped that the affected country can make provision for covering its food security requirements without jeopardising planned imports of capital goods necessary for achieving its overall development goals.

Wheat trade convention

The IMF facility provides financial assistance to help food importing ldcs to weather short-term fluctuations in domestic production and world prices. Other elements in the package aim to reduce supply or price fluctuations. The Wheat Trade Convention addresses fluctuations in the world price of wheat, which is the most important internationally traded grain. For 10 years efforts have been made, involving the EEC, to renegotiate the 1971 International Wheat Agreement (IWA) on a basis that more adequately meets the needs of food importing ldcs (see *Survey 1* Chapter 1). A new IWA, like its predecessor, would contain two elements: a wheat trade convention and a food aid convention. If negotiated, a new wheat trade convention would be the most suitable instrument for addressing the broader problem of market instability. However, there is very little likelihood that an acceptable arrangement can be achieved. Since expiry of the International Grains Agreement a decade ago, members of the Wheat Council have been attempting to devise a formula for creating and managing reserve stocks so that extreme fluctuations in market prices could be blunted. While countries have reached a concensus on the rhetoric, there have been and continue to be serious differences of philosophy about what should really be done.

The EEC has long been a proponent of regulated world markets, which would involve stocks and production control measures of sufficient magnitude to prevent world prices from fluctuating outside a fairly narrow and relatively high price band. This approach would be consistent with the operation of the CAP for grains, but it would be costly in the sense that either large stocks would have to be subsidised, or major producing countries would have to pay farmers to curtail production when prices fell to the relatively high minimum. For ldcs it might avoid the problems created by price instability, but it would not necessarily reduce the cost of grain imports, since prices would be stabilised at a somewhat higher level than now prevails. Canada and Australia both have Wheat Boards which manage the flow of domestic grain into the export market and are therefore sympathetic to the EEC's regulated market approach. Even more than the EEC, they consider that the primary benefit to themselves would come from the generally higher price level that would prevail, and they are unlikely to be very forthcoming with reserve stock undertakings or special provisions for developing countries unless their primary objective is met. If necessary they would also consider forming an exporters' cartel to achieve their aim rather than agreeing to an international system with no teeth.

The United States takes a more or less opposite view. While various

Table 2.1 *World cereal stocks, total composition and percent of world consumption 1969/70–1980/81*

	1969/70–1971/72 average	*1972/73–1973/74 average*	*1974/75–1975/76 average*	*1976/77–1977/78 average*	*1978/79–1979/80*[b] *average*	*1980/81*[b]
			(million metric tons)			
World cereal stocks[a]	225	184	175	233	254	214
Canada	27	16	13	19	18	na
China	40	40	40	41	48	48
EEC	12	13	15	12	15	na
India	15	11	11	21	18	na
USA	67	40	32	68	75	na
USSR	16	24	14	11	13	na
World cereal consumption	1142	1232	1229	1321	1437	1456
			(per cent)			
Ratio of stocks to consumption	19	15	14	18	19	15
Stocks composition[c]						
Wheat	45	46	46	48	43	44
Rice	10	9	12	11	13	14
Coarse grains	45	45	42	41	44	42

[a] Stocks data is aggregated from crop year data for individual countries, and does not represent the stock level at any particular point in time.
[b] Estimate.
[c] Assumes commodity composition for China remains constant throughout.

Sources: Stocks data for all countries except China from Foreign Agricultural Service, US Department of Agriculture. China stocks consumption data for all countries and data from Food and Agriculture Organization of the United Nations (FAO).

Table 2.2 *World cereal stocks, by major producing country,*[a] *1969/70–1979/80* (million metric tons)

	1969/70	*1970/71*	*1971/72*	*1972/73*	*1973/74*	*1974/75*	*1975/76*	*1976/77*	*1977/78*	*1978/79*	*1979/80*[b]
Developed countries	163	126	141	108	111	102	93	137	136	167	143
Australia	9	5	3	1	3	2	3	3	2	7	9
Canada	35	25	22	16	16	14	13	18	19	22	14
Eastern Europe	5	3	3	3	3	4	3	5	5	4	4
EEC	12	12	13	12	14	17	13	12	12	16	16
Japan	9	8	5	4	4	5	6	7	9	11	11
Other Europe	5	4	6	5	6	10	10	9	8	10	8
South Africa	1	1	1	2	3	2	2	3	3	2	2
USA	73	55	74	48	31	28	37	62	74	73	78
USSR	20	12	15	17	31	21	7	18	4	23	4
Developing countries	69	71	73	67	73	71	84	101	96	99	103
Argentina	1.1	1.6	0.7	1.0	1.5	1.9	1.6	1.9	1.4	1.1	0.7
Bangladesh	–	–	–	0.1	0.2	0.1	0.8	0.4	0.9	0.6	0.6
Brazil	3.7	2.3	0.9	1.1	1.0	1.2	2.0	2.3	0.7	1.0	1.6
Burma	0	0	0	0	0	0.8	1.5	1.5	1.5	0.8	1.7
China	40.0	40.0	40.0	40.0	40.0	40.0	39.3	43.0	39.0	46.0	50.5
Egypt	na	na	na	na	2.8	2.9	2.9	2.8	3.0	2.6	2.6
India	17.0	14.0	15.0	11.1	10.4	5.7	17.3	21.2	21.7	20.3	15.7
Indonesia	1.9	2.0	1.4	1.7	2.0	1.6	2.2	0.9	1.5	1.2	2.5
Iran	0.4	0.6	0.3	0.4	0.5	0.7	0.2	0.7	0.6	0.6	1.3
Korea, Rep.	1.3	0.9	1.0	0.9	0.5	1.0	0.9	1.5	1.9	1.5	2.0
Mexico	0.9	0.8	0.4	0.8	0.4	1.5	1.8	2.0	1.1	0.8	1.3
Nigeria	0	0	0	0	0	0	0	0	0	0.2	0.3
Pakistan	0.7	0.8	1.4	1.4	1.7	1.7	1.6	0.9	1.1	1.6	1.4
Philippines	0.9	0.9	1.0	1.2	0.7	0.9	1.4	1.4	1.3	1.5	1.7
Thailand	1.4	1.4	0.9	1.3	1.8	1.9	1.2	1.3	1.9	1.4	2.1
Turkey	2.1	1.3	3.3	2.3	1.2	1.3	3.0	5.4	6.3	6.0	5.2

[a] Includes all developed countries or sub-regions and all developing countries producing more than 8 million tons of cereals in 1978, except Vietnam, for which no stocks data are available.
[b] Estimate.

Sources: As Table 2.1. Production data from FAO *Production Yearbook*.

administrations have supported the concept of internationally-coordinated reserve stocks to greater or lesser degree, the USA has consistently opposed tight regulation of world market prices. To the extent that it has been willing to agree to the inclusion of price provisions in a new wheat agreement, it has insisted that the price band within which market prices could fluctuate be quite wide, and has preferred consultative mechanisms rather than prearranged rules for deciding what market action, if any, should be taken when prices approach the lower or upper bounds. At the time this *Survey* went to press, the USA had indicated it would not subject its own farmer-held reserves to any form of international coordination, preferring only to encourage other countries to join with it in building up world stocks to safe levels.

These important differences became apparent in the 1978/79 negotiations which followed the expiry of the 1971 IWA. Despite the problems and the fact that Soviet participation, though crucial, was uncertain, agreement in principle was reached by the major producers in early 1979. But then the concerns of the food importing developing countries came to the fore, and *Group of 77* spokesmen indicated that developing countries would refuse to join unless the price band was lowered or a two-tier price system created which would in effect subsidise the cost of their commercial cereal imports. Developed country food exporters took the view that these were considerations for policy on food aid and financial assistance for food security infrastructure. They were not prepared to take them into account in the debate on price and stock provisions. Negotiations on a new trade convention therefore collapsed. Since then the Wheat Council secretariat has been working to develop an alternative approach, and one was considered at a special session of the Council in March 1981. However, the participants could agree only to continue discussing it and simply to extend the Wheat Trade Convention and Food Aid Convention in their current forms from July 1981 to June 1983.

This outcome is not surprising, given the economic and political realities which the negotiators face. Nor is there much likelihood that the outlook will change perceptibly during the coming year. For one thing, the world has already made a response of sorts to the felt need for a more conscious approach to food security. In the early 1970s, a reserve of 60 million tons was considered adequate – about half wheat and half feedgrains – and a figure of 30 million tons was used as the initial target stock level when serious discussions of a new wheat agreement first began. Since then, negotiators have lowered their sights about what constitutes an adequate reserve. Yet the actual level of reserve stocks has been increasing (see Table 2.1) and while estimates differ, all sources show that global stock levels have in fact been at or above the minimum for each of the past four years, with the reserve stock element amounting to over 73 million tons at the end of the 1980 crop year according to FAO.[3] Furthermore, the proportion held by developing countries has increased, so that vulnerability to a shock in one or two major producing countries is somewhat less than it was a decade ago. Whereas developing countries, including China, held 30% of the world total in the early 1970s, their share now comes to 42% and accounts for almost all of the total growth in world stock levels (see Table 2.2).

FAO estimates that total cereal carryover should equal 17% of total consumption each year in order to provide an adequate margin of safety against crop failure the following year (about 12% as pipeline inventories or working stocks, and 5% as the reserve element). The estimated stocks drawdown in 1980/81 have brought total carryover to only around 15% of consumption going into 1981/82. At first sight this might seem to justify strengthening the food reserve element of nationally-held grain stocks to bring carryover levels up to the FAO minimum. Yet to argue thus overlooks the fact that the world has suffered two bad production years in a row, and that the drawdown of stocks, particularly of feedgrains, was a natural and appropriate response to severe maize crop losses and would presumably have been made in approximately the same fashion even had the formal price indicators and joint release procedures been operative. It is unlikely that the world will experience a third year of poor crops, nor is the approach to international food reserves contemplated by the International Wheat Council intended to cover such an eventuality. In fact, in the present situation, both acreages and yields for 1981/82 appear likely to increase substantially over the previous year, thus allowing restoration of stocks to a relatively secure level.

The current experience highlights an aspect of world food security which is frequently overlooked, but which is undoubtedly vital, namely that of future land management policies in both developed and developing countries. Even in countries where the total land area for agriculture has nearly reached its limit, this land can be used in different ways, depending on relative prices for different crops. After taking into account the time trend for area planted to wheat and coarse grains in the world as a whole, regression analysis shows that the residual variation in area planted to total cereals is highly responsive to world wheat price movements. As Table 2.3 shows, area response is greater in some countries than in others. The EEC, for example, has held area constant while increasing production substantially through improvements in yield. Nevertheless, for the world as a whole, there has been a clear area response to price movements interacting with an overall trend increase in cereals over time. If the view of pessimists were correct that the major producers have reached the outer limits of their capacity for growth through acreage and yield increases, then the prospects for rebuilding a comfortable grain stock cushion without a binding international agreement to do so would be slim. However, experience to date shows that the recovery powers of major producers in both the North and the South, including the EEC, are considerable, and the evidence thus far indicates that there has been no real long-term increase in the world price of grain, despite the increase in price variability since 1972.[4]

Table 2.3 *Area planted to wheat and maize, by major producing country, 1969/70–1980/81, and annual prices lagged two years*

	1969/70	*1970/71*	*1971/72*	*1972/73*	*1973/74*	*1974/75*	*1975/76*	*1976/77*	*1977/78*	*1978/79*	*1979/80*	*1980/81*
					(area in million hectares)							
Wheat												
Argentina	6.2	4.5	5.0	5.6	4.3	5.2	5.6	7.2	4.6	5.2	5.0	6.1
Australia	9.5	6.5	7.1	7.6	8.9	8.3	8.6	9.0	10.0	10.2	11.1	11.5
Canada	5.1	7.9	8.6	9.6	8.9	9.5	11.3	10.1	10.6	10.5	11.1	11.9
EEC	11.1	10.9	11.1	11.1	10.8	11.2	10.5	11.2	10.1	11.0	11.0	11.6
USA	19.7	21.8	22.2	24.0	28.8	30.3	32.5	30.5	26.7	28.9	32.6	35.9
India	16.6	18.2	19.1	19.5	18.6	18.0	20.5	20.9	21.5	22.2	na	na
Coarse grains												
Argentina	7.2	8.1	7.2	7.2	7.2	6.5	6.1	5.8	5.8	5.8	5.2	6.3
Australia	3.4	4.3	4.6	3.9	3.7	3.3	3.9	4.0	4.4	4.7	4.2	4.5
Canada	8.2	8.4	10.2	9.2	9.1	8.9	8.6	8.4	8.5	7.8	7.1	7.9
EEC	15.8	16.0	15.8	15.8	15.9	15.5	15.8	15.1	15.6	16.8	15.7	15.1
USA	49.7	53.6	47.8	50.3	50.2	50.7	53.1	53.4	51.4	49.2	50.3	51.3
USSR	na	na	na	na	na	91.2	95.1	96.7	na	94.2	101.8	93.0
India	47.2	45.0	43.7	42.2	46.2	43.1	43.7	42.1	42.2	42.1	na	na
World total cereals	680.9	670.4	678.9	672.6	698.2	700.4	717.4	717.7	713.3	713.4	709.1	721.1
	1968	*1969*	*1970*	*1971*	*1972*	*1973*	*1974*	*1975*	*1976*	*1977*	*1978*	
				(price in 1977 constant dollars per metric ton)								
Wheat	151	144	132	132	133	219	228	153	135	96	108	
Maize	127	138	135	125	108	157	169	132	123	95	87	

Note: For EEC, area figures are for area harvested. For Argentina, coarse grains include only maize and sorghum. For USSR, coarse grains include all spring-planted grains, including wheat, much of which is fed to livestock. For India, area figures are for area harvested and exclude rice which accounts for about a third of total cereals area and has been expanding. For world, area harvested is used as a proxy for area planted.

Sources: Area data from USDA estimates, except India which is from 'Estimates of area and production of principal crops in India 1978–9', Directorate of Economics and Statistics, Ministry of Agriculture, Government of India, 1980. Price data from World Bank *Commodity Trade and Price Trends 1978*

The new approach to negotiation of a wheat trade convention does not differ sufficiently from previous approaches to make success likely. Although reserve stocks would be nationally-held, the proposal calls for a joint decision of the International Wheat Council about acquisition and release of stocks each time actual prices move 15–20 % below or above a fixed indicator price.[5] Once taken, this decision would be binding on member countries. In practice, this procedure would be a departure from the loose consultative mechanism provided by the existing Wheat Trade Convention, and in the eyes of most would mean a sacrifice of flexibility with respect to domestic farm management policies without any compensating gain in either commercial market prospects or internal food security. Further, it is quite possible that any actual agreement would quickly break down in the face of its first real test, since the indicator prices do not automatically trigger action, and it could prove difficult for Wheat Council members with differing domestic interests to reach agreement on what stock actions or other measures should be taken. Thus reserves bound by a new convention only for release by decision of the Wheat Council would most likely either sit idle or be released in contravention of the agreed procedures. Such an arrangement would not necessarily be in the best interests of food importing ldcs for whom food security is important.

If a new wheat trade convention could be negotiated to provide market stability at current price levels, and if the reserve stocks governed by such a convention were held largely by the major producers and exporters, ldcs would of course benefit as free riders in a regulated market. However, it is not necessarily in their interest to participate in an agreement requiring them to constitute reserve stocks which can only be released in accordance with the governing rules of the International Wheat Council. Apart from the cost factor, most developing countries need to acquire and release stocks in relation to movements in domestic prices and internal markets, rather than the world market. They may be trying to administer incentive price programmes for farmers or to subsidise consumer prices, or both, and the price levels they want to maintain internally may very well be different from those which would be negotiated in an international agreement.

For many food importing developing countries, a more satisfactory line of advance lies not in a new wheat trade convention, but in the creation of international stocks of the kind proposed in the International Undertaking on World Food Security and the FAO Plan of Action on World Food Security. The Undertaking calls on countries on an individual basis to follow stock policies that, in combination, will provide food security for the world. In a recent report to the FAO Committee on World Food Security it was noted that 60 countries representing 57 % of all people in developing countries have adopted explicit stock policies and that 9 others have such policies under active consideration.[6] Many of these are aimed primarily at improving the country's management of its working stocks and pipeline inventories. Yet without this first essential step of linking price and procurement policies for domestic cereals with a conscious storage programme, most countries will not have the capacity to move toward reserve stock creation except with imported cereals and at great expense to the development of their own domestic agriculture.

Food aid

The negotiation of a new international trade agreement thus seems less crucial than it once did. An alternative to speedy resolution of a new wheat trade convention would be to broaden the other pillar of the international wheat agreement – the Food Aid Convention (FAC) – by including within its ambit other measures that would contribute specifically to ldc food security. The EEC is an important food aid donor. Its activities have been criticised on a number of grounds, and both the Commission and the Council in their pronouncements examined in the first section of this chapter, admit that the implementation of food aid can be improved. As a major participant in negotiating the FAC it can influence the form such changes take at an international level, and as an important donor in its own right it can amend its own practices. If changes are envisaged, the first question to ask is what reforms to the international system are desirable. After that, the EEC's current practice can be measured against the ideal.

One obvious reform is to link food aid more closely with reserve stocks. The Wheat Council has proposed the creation of an Assistance Evaluation Committee (AEC) as a means whereby developed country members of the Wheat Council could review the status of reserve stock creation in developing country members of a new wheat trade convention, and consider what assistance, if any, need be provided to assure that these members could meet their stock obligations. Such a committee could form an arm of the Food Aid Convention. Even without formal ldc reserve stock commitments, such a committee could play a useful role, particularly if it were backed up by a consultative group for financing food security reserves, as proposed by the executive director of the World Food Council. Further international action to assist developing countries in creating their own storage programmes is highly desirable, but at present donor efforts are all too often fragmented and conflicting. For example, the FAO food security assistance scheme (FSAS) focusses on helping low-income developing countries design reserve stock programmes in central locations which can be externally financed, created with food aid, and used to prevent urban food prices from rising when domestic procurement fails. The World Bank, on the other hand, focusses on helping countries to develop the capacity to design and manage price and procurement policies which rely on domestic production, and bases its recommendations for storage programmes on the outcome of other domestic farm and food policy decisions. In addition, a number of bilateral donors are seeking to assist ldcs to develop reserve stock programmes in various ways. Since the Bank has already indicated its readiness to cooperate with the International Wheat Council in this endeavour, and stands ready to back up its interest with a substantial commitment of funds, it seems sensible to capitalise on the Bank's initiative by bringing other donors into a consultative framework for food security assistance under the auspices of a broadened Food Aid and Food Security Convention.

Another aspect of food security toward which the Food Aid Convention could make a contribution is the continuing need for emergency assistance in the face of unexpected crop failures or other distress situations. Despite creation of the IMF food facility, there will continue to be occasions when the poorer developing countries will have exceptional requirements for food imports and will not be able to finance them. Although the current Food Aid Convention guarantees a minimum annual food aid level of 7.6 million tons, the situation is in reality no more secure than in the early 1970s when the minimum was 4.2 million tons. The problem is that although in normal years food aid flows are higher than the minimum, a period of high prices and tight supplies can lead to cutbacks in food aid, precisely when it is most needed. The current FAC does provide that its governing body may recommend that members increase the amount of aid available when there are widespread shortages in developing countries. However, this provision could be greatly strengthened by making such increases obligatory.

The kind of emergency which variable food aid commitments are intended to meet is the more generalised need for additional imports or balance of payments assistance arising from widespread production shortfalls and high market prices. The magnitude of this requirement has been variously estimated from 1 to 4 million tons in an average year, and from 12 to 16 million tons in an extreme year.[7] While the average year requirement could be met from normal food aid flows, donors are unlikely to divert large additional quantities of grain to aid recipients while commercial customers' requirements remain unmet. The World Food Council has before it a proposal that the international community consider creating a special food crisis reserve of 9 million tons. The USA's emergency food reserve of 4 million tons created expressly to back up its food aid commitments could form the first tranche of this reserve, and other donor country reserve obligations could be negotiated in accordance with their shares in a renegotiated FAC containing variable emergency food aid commitments.

These considerations add up to a requirement that food aid be guaranteed available when needed, and be accurately targeted to the areas where it can best be absorbed. This implies a donor control mechanism that is flexible, responsive to ldc needs, and able to provide the recipient with sufficient certainty about the scale and timing of deliveries that the food aid can be taken into account in food sector planning. The EEC's current practice falls far short of these requirements.

In 1981 the EEC increased its cereal food aid in line with the adoption of the new FAC minimum. The Ten provide food aid through the bilateral programmes of some member states, and through the Community. The Community-level programme covers virtually all the dairy products supplied as food aid, but only some 56% of the cereals (which are mainly wheat, maize, maize meal and rice). Under the new FAC, the Ten will provide 22% of the total minimum committment of cereals, or 1650,000 tons, but of this only 927,663 tons will be channelled through the Community institutions while the remaining 722,337 tons will be administered by the member states in their bilateral programmes. The Community-level cereal commitment is 29% higher than the level that has applied since 1976 (see Table 2.4). In the view of the Commission this increase is not adequate, given its estimate of the demand for food aid in the Third World. There has been no parallel increase in the non-cereal food aid programme, which is not covered by the FAC and which consists largely of dried skim milk and butteroil (a processed form of butter which is much less perishable). The dairy products programme has remained at the same level since 1976 (see Table 2.5).

Criticisms of the EEC's Community-level food aid are levelled less at the quantity supplied than at the quality of the system for providing and monitoring assistance. In 1979/80 the EEC Court of Auditors undertook a major study of the implementation of EEC food aid, published in 1981. The Court's Report is undoubtedly the most comprehensive 'inside' analysis of the objectives and results of EEC food aid. Although it found that mishaps in the administration of food aid were the exception rather than the rule, it concluded that thoroughgoing reforms are required to overcome institutionalised weaknesses. Among these weaknesses, it identified the extreme complexity, slowness, and fragmentation of EEC procedures. The average delay between the proposal of a programme and the unloading of the food at a port in Asia is 377 days for cereals, and 535 days for milk products. As a result, food aid often reaches the recipient too late or at an inconvenient time. The Court also found that the Commission often failed to recognise the practical difficulties facing the recipient countries, or their real needs.

At the root of these problems is the fact that the EEC is pursuing three mutually incompatible policies that result in muddled logistics, and reduce the capacity of the system to relate to ldc needs. The three policies are:

- the provision of food aid on an annual basis so that the Council of Ministers can retain responsibility not only for setting each year the volume of commodities to be provided, but also their precise distribution between recipient states. Since the adoption of each year's programme is the result of haggling between the Commission and the

Council, recipient countries find it difficult to plan because they have no certainty whether their bid for an allocation in any year will be successful, or if it is, what quantity they will receive or when it will be delivered.

the distribution of food aid to a large number of countries, often in very small consignments. For the cereals programme, there are two groups: a small group of very large recipients, and a large group of small recipients. In the 1980 programme, for example, commitments to the top three recipients (Bangladesh, Egypt and Pakistan) totalled 54% of the direct food aid, while the figure for the top eleven recipients was 78%.[8] Since there were a total of 37 country allocations, it follows that the remaining 26 recipients shared a mere 22% of the programme and often had allocations of only 1000–2000 tons.

– this annually agreed, dispersed programme is administered by a very small staff which is fragmented between several organisations. Overall responsibility inside the EEC Commission lies with the food aid division of DG8, which numbers only some 20 staff, but the task of organising the supply and transport of food aid commodities is shared with the directorate-general for agriculture (DG6) and also intervention boards of member states, whose prime task is to dispose of EEC production, not to ensure the well-being of food importing ldcs.

None of these three policies, taken by itself, is necessarily undesirable or need limit the value of EEC food aid to the recipient. Taken together, however, they cause confusion, uncertainty and lack of control, and their net result is to reduce the extent to which ldcs can benefit from EEC food aid. Although the problems appear superficially to be administrative ones, in reality they result from a political decision to maintain these three policies. It lies, therefore, with the Council of Ministers to agree changes that would reduce the problems. In November 1980, the Council took a decision to open up the possibility of multi-annual programming for a 'reasonable proportion' of the total programme. The Commission has expressed its intentions to make use of this provision in the 1981 programme and to put forward proposals on a case-by-case basis for multi-annual commitments to support development projects in some recipient states. Hence, the actual impact of the Council's policy decision will depend upon its attitude to the case-by-case proposals of the Commission, and it will not become clear how liberally the policy will be interpreted until a body of 'case law' is built up in 1982 and beyond. In the meantime, a partial improvement can be obtained by channelling Community-level aid through intergovernmental and non-governmental organisations such as the World Food Programme, Red Cross and Catholic Relief Services. It then becomes the responsibility of these third parties and not of the recipient ldcs, to remove the uncertainties and lack of control inherent in the EEC system. Third party intermediaries are

Table 2.4 *Size of the EEC cereals food aid programme 1968/69–1980/81*

	1968/69	*1969/70*	*1970/71*	*1971/72*	*1972/73*	*1973/74*	*1974/75*	*1975/76*	*1976/77*	*1977/78*	*1978/79*	*1979/80*	*1980/81*
Quantities (in tonnes)													
Community actions	301 000	337 000	353 000	414 000	464 000	580 000	643 500	708 000	720 500	720 500	720 500	720 500	927 663
National actions	734 000	698 000	682 000	621 000	696 000	707 000	643 500	579 000	566 500	566 500	566 500	566 500	722 337
	1035 000	1035 000	1035 000	1035 000	1160 000	1287 000	1287 000	1287 000	1287 000	1287 000	1287 000	1287 000	1650 000
Value in world prices (in million uc)[a]													
Community actions	19.6	21.9	30.7	29.4	71.0	110.2	86.87	97.97	82.20	88.80	96.12	111.06	na
National actions	47.7	45.4	59.3	44.1	106.6	134.3	86.87	80.12	64.63	69.81	75.57	87.32	na
	67.3	67.3	90.0	73.5	177.6	244.5	173.74	178.09	146.83	158.61	171.69	198.38	na

[a] Million Eua since 1978.

Source: EEC Commission.

Table 2.5 *Size of the EEC non-cereals food aid programme 1970–1981*

	1970	*1971*	*1972*	*1973*	*1974*	*1975*	*1976*	*1977*	*1978*	*1979*	*1980*	*1981*
Quantities (in tonnes)												
Milk	127 000	–	60 000	13 000	55 000	55 000	150 000	150 000	150 000	150 000	150 000	150 000
Butteroil	37 000	–	15 000	–	45 000	45 000	45 000	45 000	45 000	45 000	45 000	45 000
Eggs	–	–	500	–	–	–	–	–	–	–	–	na
Sugar	–	–	6 150	6 062	6 094	–	6 094	6 153	6 153	6 153	8 086	na
Value in world prices (in million uc)[a]												
Milk	73.4	–	39.1	8.9	46.0	30.2	76.98	41.50	76.05	87.94	109.95	na
Butteroil	57.9	–	19.6	–	61.1	64.1	68.95	47.00	56.34	62.25	67.83	na
Eggs	–	–	1.2	–	–	–	–	–	–	–	–	na
Sugar	–	–	1.6	1.9	3.7	–	2.33	1.70	1.52	1.45	2.00	na
Contributions in cash[b]	–	–	1.6	1.6	3.8	3.0	1.00	1.00	1.00	0.50	57.86	na
	131.3	–	63.1	12.4	114.6	97.3	149.26	91.20	134.91	152.14	237.64	

[a] Million Eua since 1978.
[b] From 1980 onwards this line includes transport costs itemised individually in the budget.

Source: EEC Commission.

used by the EEC more frequently with dairy products than with cereals, reflecting differences in the ease with which the two commodities can be absorbed by ldcs. Under the 1981 programme, 18 % of the cereals, but a full 40 % of the milk and 30 % of the butter are earmarked for international organisations.

EEC aid to ldc agricultural production

Measures to increase world food security by enabling countries to obtain from the world market the food that they need are a complement to efforts to increase food production in food deficit ldcs. Indeed there is a widespread view (with which both the Commission and the Council concur in their declared policy) that increasing ldc food production is the primary goal, and that measures such as food aid are only acceptable if they do not detract from efforts to attain it. Many of the changes required to increase ldc food production involve domestic reforms and innovations, and are the responsibility of the ldcs themselves. The industrialised world can support this process by helping to create an environment that facilitates such domestic reform, and by providing assistance to agricultural development projects. Both the Commission and the Council policy statements reviewed in the first part of this chapter place a high priority on increasing the volume of aid for agricultural development projects, and on improving the ways in which it is given.

The phrase 'increasing ldc food production' is often tossed-off as if the task were a simple matter involving a few key policy decisions. In practice, it is very complex, and the obstacles to success are numerous. The same applies to aid to assist food and agricultural development schemes. There are great variations between different parts of the Third World, and the situation is by no means entirely gloomy. However, the question of how far aid has actually fostered ldc agriculture has to be asked with particular force of the EEC aid programme. This is because EEC aid has been focussed on Africa under the Lomé and Yaoundé conventions, and Africa is the region of the Third World in which recent production trends have been the most disappointing and the outlook is most gloomy. FAO figures for Africa as a whole, suggest that food production grew, over the period 1969–78 at 1.6 % per annum. Set against annual rates of population growth in the range 2.0 – 3.5 % or more, this means that per capita food production is estimated to have decreased by 1.3 % per annum. During 1978, 26 countries faced abnormal food shortages reaching crisis proportions; of these 17 were in Africa. Not unnaturally, this had led to a substantial increase in food imports into Africa. The volume of grain imported into Africa has grown from an annual average 2.895 million tonnes in 1961–65 to 9.271 million tonnes in 1976–78. Thus, in Africa at least, the aid programmes of the past decade have not succeeded in increasing per capita food production.

Clearly there are factors external to aid programmes which are responsible for much of this failure, but there are also a number of ways in which aid programmes themselves can impede rather than assist the development of food production and especially the availability of food to the poorer sections of the populations. First, they may divert attention away from solution of the most pressing agricultural needs. The real problem is to increase food production in such a way that the extra food produced gets to (or stays with) those who need it most, that is, the poorest sections of the rural and urban populations. This is not necessarily something that foreign aid can achieve easily. It is simplistic to assume that the development of cash crops for export or for consumption by local elites is always harmful to the interests of the poor, but it is true that there is a tendency for aid to be concentrated on cash crops and on large-scale machinery-intensive projects, and that, given the limited implementation capacity of ldcs, this emphasis may lead to a neglect of programmes that would benefit the poor more directly. More generally, given very fragile administrative structures and material infrastructure in most ACP states, the imposition of successive layers of aid projects, each with its own administrative requirements and needs for transport, construction inputs, agricultural inputs, skilled labour, credit and research, can have serious effects upon the remainder of the economy and notably upon the peasant sector.

Moreover, there is a tendency for official opinion to see the problem as being primarily *technical* and *financial*, requiring a major increase in the funds allocated to development projects which should be primarily concerned with increasing productivity through the application of more 'modern' agricultural methods. Current thinking seems to favour improved seeds, fertilizers and insecticides more than tractors, though the latter are still prominent in proposals and much more so in actual spending. Yet fertilizers, by themselves, do not always increase crop yields. They have to be used properly, at the right time, within a suitable system of cultivation and, even then, one has to hope for good weather. Still less is it always the case that fertilizer use pays for itself, given the price and quality of some fertilizers available to Third World farmers. Similarly it may seem a verbal quibble to note that a tractor, on its own, can do little more than rust – until one has seen large numbers of tractors doing just that and nothing else. Mechanised agriculture requires not only considerable amounts of skilled and incentivised labour but crucially it needs a high degree of organisation which inevitably will require local trained personnel, often of those sorts most lacking, and will usually have to be grafted on to some existing administrative structure whose other functions may be different in nature or at cross-purposes with the one to be achieved.

Given these constraints, how does EEC aid to agriculture measure up to the problems? First, it should be noted that despite the Community's claims that aid to agriculture should increase, commitments from the

Table 2.6 *EDF and EIB commitments to rural production* (Eua mn)

	Rural Production		*Total*		*Rural Production*
	Current prices	*Constant 1976 prices*	*Current prices*	*Constant 1976 prices*	*as a % of total*
1976	89	89	446	446	20
1977	192	177	775	714	25
1978	106	85	673	538	16
1979	105	74	688	484	15
1980	84	53	579	366	15

Notes: Although the time period covers the duration of Lomé I, commitments are not just from EDF IV but are also from EDFs I–III.

Source: EEC Commission.

European Development Fund (EDF) to the African, Caribbean and Pacific (ACP) signatories of Lomé conventions show no evidence of this. Table 2.6 shows commitments from the EDF and EIB for the period 1976–1980 both in total and the proportion earmarked for rural production (fuller figures on the sectoral breakdown of EDF aid are in the Statistical Appendix). Commitments to rural production have fallen over the period on all counts: in current prices, in constant prices and as a proportion of total commitments. Furthermore, as explained in *Survey 1* (Chapter 3) aid flows under Lomé II will be some 20 % below those of Lomé I in real, per capita terms. The Commission itself uses a different definition of the proportion of funds going to the rural sector, which includes a certain proportion of economic and social infrastructure. While this may be justified for some purposes, it does not alter the fact that the amounts directed to rural production have declined both proportionately and in absolute terms. However, this problem of definition does highlight the fact that aggregate categories of aid spending are not particularly helpful. Unfortunately, the standard breakdown used by the EEC for the allocation of funds within the 'rural production' category conceals as much as it reveals (see Table 2.7). Given the importance of vague catch-all categories like 'general' and 'agriculture' and the fact that hydro-agricultural projects may range from small peasant-oriented irrigation schemes to vast hydro-electric schemes with associated mechanised farming, this tells little about how the funds were spent. Commission sources are concerned to imply that the major proportion goes to peasant-oriented schemes, and a trend in this direction seems apparent from the replacement of plantations by integrated projects as the largest single category. However it is much less certain that this represents a move towards more direct concern with the production of basic foodstuffs.

Table 2.7 *Allocation of EDF and EIB Funds within Rural Production category (Eua mn) 1976–79*

	1976	*1977*	*1978*	*1979*
General	0.8	19.2	9.3	9.3
Plantations	43.3	43.6	11.2	16.4
Hydro-Agric. Projects	15.4	29.0	11.0	3.4
Agriculture	21.3	54.4	24.7	11.9
Livestock Farming	3.2	11.7	15.3	5.6
Fisheries	4.8	2.2	2.0	4.0
Forestry	–	3.5	0.1	1.4
Microprojects	0.3	6.5	9.2	5.3
Integrated Projects	–	21.5	23.0	43.9
Total	89.0	191.6	103.8	101.3

In view of this lack of precision in official classification, an alternative breakdown has been made on the basis of individual project titles (and descriptions where given) and funds committed, as reported in *The Courier* for most of the period covered by Tables 2.6 and 2.7. In some senses, this is a cruder classification than that used by the Commission since it is not possible to include parts of specific projects (say credit which is for both agricultural and non-agricultural use), to exclude parts of others (some processing) or to distinguish between years. Moreover, as with the Commission reports, many project titles are far from illuminating. Nevertheless, the exercise does allow the classification of a large proportion of projects according to potential beneficiary and type of product involved. Table 2.8 shows (by column) the proportion of funds going to large farms and plantations, small and medium farms, services to and research for the agricultural sector and 'unspecified'. The rows show proportions to export crops, 'food crops', 'unspecified crops', livestock, forestry and fisheries.

Interpretation is complicated by the fact that the largest single product category is 'unspecified crops', while 'unspecified farm size' is also large. But one thing is certain: Table 2.8 does not bear out any claim to a primary emphasis on food crops. First, much of the 'crops not specified' category concerns integrated projects, which are commonly focussed around one or more export crops. Second, the category 'food crops' is not solely concerned with basic staple foods – investment in sugar plantations alone takes over a quarter of total spending in this category, while rice, wheat and fresh vegetables for export or local elites are also prominent. Apart from this, the breakdown omits investment (mostly from EIB) in processing facilities for export crops and for sugar (except where included with plantation development), which take an amount equivalent to another quarter of the total included in the table. Finally, the largest single expenditure within the food crop category is for a massive cassava

Table 2.8 *Breakdown of EDF and EIB aid flows to ACP Rural Sector Production (Per cent of total, 1977–early 1981)*

	Farm Size				
Sub-Sector	*Large*	*Small*	*Service*	*Non-Spec.*	*Total*
Export crops	12	11	..	5	28
Food crops	10	3	1	7	21
Not Specified (Crops)	7	19	3	10	39
Livestock	2	..	3	3	7
Forestry	1	–	–	2	2
Fisheries	–	..	1	1	2
Total	31	34	8	27	

Notes: Totals do not add due to rounding.
Groundnuts are considered here as an export crop since the context makes clear that this is the intention of the projects in most cases.
– equals zero.
.. equals negligible.

Source: *The Courier*

production programme, which appears to be aimed primarily at the European cattle-feed market.

Similarly, the table fails to provide firm support for EEC claims concerning the nature of the beneficiaries, such as that 1.3 million people have benefitted and that 'almost all these projects directly affected small family farms'.[9] The second claim would seem to include those expelled from their land to make way for plantations, ranches and integrated settlement schemes.

All this leaves unanswered the most important questions of all: what were the effects of the different projects, to what extent did they achieve their stated aims, how relevant to food production and availability were these and how did they affect production and marketing outside the projects themselves? For such questions, the best available source is a 1979 study of ten integrated rural development projects which were sufficiently advanced by 1976, when the field survey was performed, to make evaluation realistic.[10] Because of this, all of the countries concerned were francophone. Of the ten different countries and programmes considered, five were centred upon cotton production, two on coffee and one each on rice and groundnuts. While all contained some formal commitment to increasing food production, there was only one which appeared centred upon this aim. For several of the cotton projects, it appeared that food crops were largely ignored by the extension staff either because they were linked to the cotton purchasing agency, or because they had no useful advice to offer in relation to food crops, or both. Nonetheless, it was generally the case that, in the years up to 1977, food crop production increased more rapidly than that of cotton. The reason for this seems primarily to have been the impact of drought in 1974–75 and its impact on both crop prices and peasant concern for food security. The impression prevails from most of the studies that the peasants were responsive to market opportunities, so long as these did not require major changes in the pattern of production. Major changes in methods of cultivation were, naturally enough, harder to achieve, while soil conservation seems to have had little impact. A general impression is of excessive concentration by project administrations upon the central export crop, offset by price response and food requirements. Another point is the heavy dependence of such projects upon the standards of local administration and training and the major constraints imposed by its failures to fulfil its role. In this connection, efforts were made in several cases to set up cooperatives for the purchase of crops and supply of credit and inputs, most of which were not especially successful. While there is no special reason to suppose these projects to have been less successful than those of other agencies, they certainly do not indicate any strong emphasis on food crop production although several would appear in statistical tables as being so concerned. However since this study refers to the period up to 1977, it is possible that there may have been some change since then.

Developing country agricultural exports: the case of sugar

One of the recommendations of the Commission's May 1981 Communication on North-South which the Council failed to adopt was to urge that 'developing countries' exports of agricultural products are given improved access to the industrialised countries' consumer markets and, hence, to the European Community market'.[11] As is made clear in Chapter 3, the CAP forms a protective barrier that excludes from the EEC market most ldc agricultural exports that compete directly with domestic production. However, for various reasons a few competitive ldc commodities have found a niche in the EEC market. Such concessions tend to be for relatively small amounts, but they may be very valuable for the exporting states. Because they compete with domestic EEC production, they are vulnerable to pressure from the agricultural lobbies. Moreover, at times when the CAP is undergoing change, they are particularly vulnerable. Hence, exports of fruit, vegetables and oil from the southern mediterranean will be put at risk by the enlargement of the Community (and the scope of the CAP) to include Spain and Portugal (see *Survey 1*, Chapter 4). Similarly, some of the proposals put forward by the Commission for reform of the CAP, which are reviewed in Chapter 3, have serious implications for ldc agricultural exports. For this reason, the experience of ldc exports that currently have access to the EEC market has a significance that far outweighs the importance of the commodities themselves because it illustrates the forces that are at work to maintain or to remove the concessions, and hence provides a guide to the likely impact of CAP reforms on ldc agricultural exporters. Probably the most important concession under the CAP is that provided to the cane sugar exporting signatories of the Lomé Convention plus India. Under the sugar protocol annexed to the Lomé Conventions the EEC has agreed to import annually 1.3 million tons of cane sugar at the prices prevailing for domestic beet sugar.

The case of sugar is important because of the quantities involved, the significance of the commodity to many of the ACP exporting states and, particularly, because in 1980/81 the concession has been under severe pressure. The background to the sugar protocol is explained in *Survey 1* (pp. 11–15, and 48–50). In a nutshell, it was negotiated as a condition of UK membership of the EEC to protect the developing countries that had traditionally exported sugar to Britain under the Commonwealth Sugar Agreement. Such protection was necessary because the other EEC member states obtained the bulk of their sugar from beet grown inside the Community, whereas the British market traditionally has been shared between the two types of sugar. Since the UK joined the EEC, competition from beet in the British market has increased due to growing imports from continental beet producers and to a major increase in domestic beet production due to the stimulus provided by the CAP. As a result, the commitment to import 1.3 million tons of cane sugar (95 % of which is consumed in UK) is under severe pressure. There is no likelihood that the sugar protocol will be abrogated. Rather, the danger is that it will, in the words of UK industrial consumers of sugar, 'wither on the vine'. During 1980/81 there were three events that may, in retrospect, appear as milestones on this path. One was the adoption by the Council of a new sugar beet regime for 1981–86 maintaining production quotas at levels only slightly lower than those in force since 1975. The second, linked to this, was the decision by Tate and Lyle to close one of its cane sugar refineries. Third was the decision to accord cane exporters a price increase that was lower than that agreed for beet.

Under the CAP sugar beet regime, EEC producers are guaranteed market prices that are in general substantially higher than world market levels, but this guarantee applies only to a fixed quota. The level of quotas is set at roughly five year intervals. In 1975 a regime was established that was due to expire on June 30 1980. However, the Nine could not agree on the level of quotas for a new quinquennium, and so the existing regime was extended for a further year. In September 1980, the Commission produced a revised proposal for the new regime[12] which, in an amended form, was adopted by the Council of Ministers in February 1981 as the basis for beet production for the quinquennium from July 1 1981.

The Commission's proposals of September 1980 were the third set it had put forward as a basis for the next quinquennium. Each set sought to reduce the quota of sugar that benefits from full guaranteed prices on the grounds that supply exceeds demand. But precisely because the Commission was proposing cuts, the Council had difficulty agreeing to a new regime, and so each time the Commission revised its proposals it increased the size of the suggested quota. The details of the new regime, the 1975–81 regime, and the Commission's earlier proposal are provided in the Box. The two features of most significance for cane exporters are that the beet quota is set at a level the cane producers claim is too high, and that there has been an important shift in the status of cane sugar in the EEC market.

The new level of quotas

The level of beet quotas is very important for the cane industry. When supply exceeds demand there is competition for markets between the two sources of supply and, because of the way in which prices are determined, the beet industry is able to undercut cane and increase its market share. As it operates at present, the sugar protocol depends heavily on one private sector company, Tate and Lyle, to refine the bulk of the imported cane. Tate and Lyle claim, with justification, that the commercial viability of this processing depends critically on the level of beet production, and that the levels established under the 1975 regime were too high. The company was happy with the quota cuts originally proposed by the Commission for the new quinquennium (centre column in the table in the Box) arguing that 'they would have given the company the best chance to continue to operate profitably at the present level of refining capacity'. In an independent analysis of the proposal as it affected UK, a House of Lords select committee also concluded that the new quotas were 'pitched at about the right level'.[13] Unfortunately, the Council could not accept these quotas, and the levels finally agreed in February 1981 are much higher (see Box). The global quota (A and B for all of the Nine) has been reduced slightly from the 1975–81 level of 11,648,000 tonnes to 11,438,000 tonnes. However, the balance between the A and B quotas has been altered so that, as far as the UK 'A' quota is concerned, there is no change.

Tate and Lyle responded quickly to these new levels. In 1980, after publication of the Commission's final proposal, it announced the closure of its Liverpool refinery. This is the fourth refinery it has closed since 1978 with a total loss of capacity of 950,000 tons. It now retains refineries only at London and Greenock with a combined total capacity of 1.04 million tonnes. The company claims that, by making use of spare capacity in continental cane refineries, this is sufficient for refining ACP sugar. It also claims that the remaining refineries are commercially viable. Nonetheless, when combined with other pressures being exerted on cane sugar imports, the outlook is ominous.

The EEC Sugar Beet Regime

The Quotas

There are three levels of quota. Under the 1975–81 regime 'A' quotas set the quantity of beet production on which farmers received full price support; 'B' quotas represented an additional quantity for which price support was given but on which farmers and processors were required to pay a production levy to help meet the cost of export subsidies; and 'C' quotas covered any production in excess of the 'A' and 'B' limits, which received no price support and had to be sold on the world market at the going rate. In the 1981–86 regime, the three levels of quota are maintained, but the incidence of the production levy is different, as explained below.

Commission Proposals

The Commission's first proposal for a new regime was made in November 1979. In response to the Council's reaction, this was amended as part of the Commission's agricultural price proposals for 1980/81. This revised proposal was rejected by the Council, and hence a third proposal was made in September 1980. The regime agreed by the Council in February 1981 is based substantially on this third proposal although there has been a small increase in the global A quota to benefit Italy. The main points of contention in the various proposals were: the global quantity that would receive price support; the distribution of this global amount between the member states, and between the A and B quotas; and the financial responsibility of producers for the cost of disposing of surplus production. The chart below shows the solutions to these issues in the 1975–81 regime, the Commission's second proposal, which was rejected by the Council, and the agreed new regime. For simplicity, only the UK quota is given in addition to the global quota since the market for cane sugar is mainly in the UK. Figures for quotas are in thousand tonnes of white sugar equivalent; for purposes of comparison they apply to the Nine, and exclude Greece. The Commission's rejected proposal is highlighted because it was accepted by the cane producers and processors as a regime that they could live with.

	1975–81 regime	*Commission's rejected proposal*	*New regime*[a]
Global 'A' quota	9136	8697	9226
of which UK	1040	936	1040
Global 'B' quota	2512	1897	2212
of which UK	286	74	104
Producer levy	Levy on 'B' quota only	Levy on 'B' quota only	Fixed 2% levy on A and B quotas, plus a variable levy on 'B' quotas.

[a] Quotas will be reviewed for the 1984/85 and 1985/86 production years.

Price fixing for beet and cane

The production of white sugar from beet is a continuous process. Under the EEC regime a price is fixed for white sugar which is then arbitrarily divided into the price applying to the various stages of production and processing. The price paid for cane sugar is derived from these beet prices. It is not a negotiated price and neither is it related to production costs. Since there is no equivalent beet product to raw cane, the price is estimated by the cost of various stages along the beet processing chain. The result is to bias costs in favour of the beet refining industry, since it takes no account of the differences involved. A major difference is that cane sugar is split into three stages: growing and milling in the producing state; shipping; and refining from raw to white sugar in the EEC. This split process involves extra costs of transport, handling and energy (the raw crystals must be melted before refining can begin). In addition, the physical characteristics of the two industries differ. For example, cane refineries are located at port sides, bulk handling is an intermediate step, etc. The actual processing is undertaken by commercial firms (mainly Tate & Lyle which supplies the UK market) which thus have set for them by the EEC the price of their raw material and the price at which the finished product sells. Their operating margin is the difference between the two, and is the same as that available to beet processors. However, because of the extra costs involved at the refining stage for cane they are handicapped when competing with beet refiners for market shares.

The status of cane imports

Under the 1975–81 regime, B quota sugar was subject to a levy, split between the farmers and the refiners, to contribute towards the cost of subsidising exports on to the world market. The levy was imposed on surplus production which was defined as total EEC consumption minus cane imports. In other words, the arrangement acknowledged that cane imports had a legitimate share of the market, and that any beet production in excess of the beet share of the market was surplus. Under the new regime, there has been a change in the incidence of the levies. Because the Council failed to agree cuts in the quotas of a sufficient magnitude to reduce supply to the level of domestic demand, the EEC will continue to export sugar for which producers receive price support. Since world market prices will usually be lower than those in the Community, export subsidies will continue to be necessary. There are two problems with this. First, there is a budgetary problem for the EEC. Second, the effects of large, subsidised sales by the EEC on the world market have generally been considered destabilising and detrimental to the interests of other sugar exporters. The UK House of Lords described the EEC's export policy as 'one of selfishness and cynicism'.[14] A cut in A and B quotas would have solved both problems. The Council could not agree to this, and so the system of levies has been changed as an alternative method of solving the budgetary problem, while leaving the wider export problem unresolved.

The EEC's decision to address its own internal problem while leaving the wider issue unresolved has general implications for ldc sugar producers. However, in addition the method of calculating the EEC producers' levy has a particular significance for the concessional cane imports. A new flat rate 2% levy is to be imposed on A quota sugar, and in addition there will be a variable levy on B quotas. Combined, the levies are designed to cover the cost of surplus disposal. The important point for the cane producers is that there has been a subtle shift in the basis for calculating 'surplus' production. The levies are to be set at a rate that will cover the cost of all exports *minus* 1.3 million tons representing cane imports. Under this arrangement, therefore, surplus beet production is defined as production in excess of total EEC sugar consumption not, as before, total consumption less cane imports. There has been a subtle shift in the status of cane, to emphasise that it is a *concession* and not a legitimate, long-term source of supply. Arising from this is the specific issue of how the cost of exporting the remaining 1.3 million tons will be met. This will be decided for the first time in the 1982 budget, but will remain an issue in future. Even if it is decided this year that it should be borne by the agriculture and not by the development budget, this decision may be changed in future budgets. As noted in Chapter 3, one of the proposals for 'reform' of the CAP is to transfer to other budget heads some of the expenditure currently debited to agriculture.

ACP-EEC rift over prices

In addition to the change of status for cane, the EEC decision on levies has had another effect on the cane exporters. Under the sugar protocol, the price which the exporting countries will receive for the 1.3 million tons of cane is 'negotiated' annually. The word negotiated is put in inverted commas because the process normally involves the EEC stating the price on a take-it-or-leave-it basis. However, until 1981 the price offered was always increased at the same rate that had been agreed by the EEC farm ministers for beet producers. In 1981 this link was broken. The EEC's pricing system was designed in relation to beet sugar. Since beet production is a continuous process, the practice has been to set a price for the final product – white sugar – and to derive from this the relevant prices for intermediate stages. For the first time in 1981, the Community agreed one price increase of 8.5% to apply to white sugar, and another of 7.5% to apply to raw sugar; since only the cane exporters produce raw sugar as an identifiable product, this lower rate of increase applies only to them.

There were two reasons for the introduction of a differential, both of which were related to the EEC's failure to control excess beet production. The stated reason was that although the EEC producers' price was increased by 8.5%, they were required to pay the 2% 'A' quota levy, so that their 'take-home' increase was only 6.5 %. The sugar protocol does not permit the EEC to apply differential price increases for refined beet and refined cane sugar; hence the need to invent a new way of determining the raw sugar price. The cane exporters protested vehemently that it was unreasonable for their price to be affected because of a levy designed to pay for subsidising exports of EEC surplus sugar (in competition, moreover, with the cane producers' other exports). At the time this *Survey* went to press, these protests had failed to produce any change in the EEC position and seemed unlikely to do so. This may have been because of the second, and less publicly stated reason, for introduction of the differential which was to give Tate and Lyle a greater operating margin to improve the commercial viability of cane refining despite the Community's decision not to reduce beet production significantly.

Could cane exporters de-link?

For historical reasons, the beneficiaries of the sugar protocol, especially the ACP cane exporters many of which are small, island economies, are heavily dependent upon a market and a private sector firm over which they have little influence. Their position in the EEC market is being eroded, and the cane refiners, their main ally in lobbying the EEC governments (in particular the UK), are losing their influence relative to the beet lobby. The question which arises is how far the cane producers can break out of this dependent relationship.

The answer is that they have little room for manoevre. A case has been put forward that if EEC-based cane refineries contract further, the ACP should establish their own refining industries. The technical analysis of this proposition is presented in the Box on page 44; the conclusion is that such refineries would not be viable. Not only will the ACP remain dependent upon EEC-based refineries, but they are also likely to remain heavily dependent on the EEC market. The world market for sugar is a residual market accounting for only 15 % of world production. Most traded sugar is exported under preferential arrangements similar to those of the EEC's sugar protocol. As a result, the world market is very unstable. The EEC has contributed to this instability through its subsidised exports. The Community is not a member of the International Sugar Agreement which seeks to reduce instability. Members are required to accept quotas on their exports, and this the EEC has thus far refused to do.

The situation of the ACP sugar exporters has relevance for other agricultural exporting states and for some of the proposed reforms of the CAP. It is also relevant to the discussion of other trade relations between the ldcs and the EEC, particularly the outward processing arrangements described in Chapter 7. The trade in cane sugar developed because it was in the interests of various groups in the Community that it should. Now, the balance of interests inside the Community is changing and, with it, the fortunes of the cane exporters.

The feasibility of establishing sugar refineries in the ACP

There are two elements to the feasibility of the ACP establishing their own refineries: the internal technical/financial feasibility of such refineries; and the availability of markets.

Costs of refining

Costs tend to depend upon location and scale. On most counts, location favours ACP refining, but scale may be a problem. Although many smaller establishments have been set up in developing countries, plant producers generally quote 400 tonnes per day as the minimum viable size of a refinery. There are significant economies of scale: the ratio of costs to capacity falls from 1 to less than 0.6 for capacities from 400 to 1,200 tonnes per day with variations with the particular system used. Labour and other costs will also generally vary between locations and between different designs of plant, but typically costs per tonne of output fall in a similar way with scale of production – for the range considered here (400–1,200 tpd), from about 1 to 0.46. Between 60 and 100 workers will be required overall (three shifts). This does not include 'day' workers – highly skilled, technical and scientific staff as well as management which would increase this number to between 95 and 118. Wage costs per tonne are thus highly scale related since the numbers of scientific and management staff required will increase very little with capacity, and other staff certainly less than proportionately. This is important since labour is certainly the major cost item per tonne for cane refineries in developing countries, perhaps accounting for 50% of overall running costs, and will vary between locations. Energy costs are also highly location dependent – both between countries and within countries. For example, if a refinery is added to an existing raw sugar factory, energy costs may be substantially reduced since there may be surplus bagasse (the vegetable waste discarded once the cane is crushed) to be burnt as fuel and because one stage of the process (crystallisation followed by remelting) may be omitted. From data extracted from developed countries (high energy cost regions), energy costs vary from between one quarter and three quarters of labour costs per tonne (high labour cost areas).

Because of the small size of many ACP sugar producers, there is a tension between location and scale. Considerations of scale would suggest that a large refinery be established at a point of optimal access for several raw factories, probably from several countries. Moreover, European cane refiners have always stressed the importance of the range of sources for sugar, firstly because diverse supply locations minimises the risk of crop failure, and secondly because individual crop qualities vary and a mixture helps to ensure consistently high standards. In addition, geographically diverse suppliers will ensure a reasonably steady flow of the raw commodity, spanning the various seasons. If the supply is not continuous throughout the year, then storage facilities will be necessary. However, many advisers in developed countries consider a refinery to be a viable proposition only when it is added to an existing sugar factory. This avoids intermediate transport and handling costs and may also save energy costs as noted above. But it limits possible economies of scale since raw factory sizes are restricted by the need for harvested cane to be processed within 48 hours.

Despite these problems, it is probable that in internal technical/financial terms, cane sugar refining may be feasible at least for selected ACP states.

Possible markets

The main obstacle to ACP refineries is the absence of an obvious, stable market for their output. In particular, it is very doubtful that ACP refined sugar could retain cane's share of the EEC market if the Community lost its capacity to refine the 1.3 million tonnes. Transport costs for refined sugar are extremely high. As a final consumption good, hygiene precautions must be strict and as a highly hygroscopic commodity, its handling in humid conditions carefully regulated. Whereas sugar is generally transported in bulk and loaded onto ships mechanically, the loading of refined sugar is highly labour intensive and ship turnaround time may increase fourfold. Moreover, many exporters (and EEC importers) of raw cane have invested in mechanised raw handling facilities at the portside which would be inappropriate for refined sugar. The appropriate packaging increases both volume and weight per tonne of sugar by more than the weight lost in refining (approximately 10 %) and thereby increases costs. In the EEC (and in USA) the principal growth in demand for sugar is coming from industry rather than final consumers. To produce sugar for industrial use demands a wide range of final products – particularly in liquid sugars which are more costly to transport. Because of their distance from the market, ACP refiners would not be able to compete effectively with beet for these markets. Moreover, in the face of declining domestic supplies, it is expected that alternative sweetners such as high fructose corn syrup (HFCS) will appear increasingly cost effective (in spite of EEC quota restrictions) and will be used.

Major sales to the USA are unlikely. As an alternative, the ACP could look to the world market. However, on the world market the margin of refined over raw prices is very small (well under 10 %), and at certain times the refined price has slipped below the raw. Many factors serve to distort these figures, but one factor must certainly be the presence of European and Russian white sugar, comprising approximately one quarter of the market.

Refining for a purely domestic market will be limited by scale economies and the unsophisticated nature of the market in many ACP countries, and would also entail changes in the domestic price regime currently imposed by many ACP sugar producing states. However, a closer look at demand patterns and trade flows suggests that refining and trading cane sugar may be profitable for several producers within localised trading spheres. Many developing countries have set up refineries, and the World Bank as well as commercial concerns have financed such projects. Increased demand is likely to come from developing countries and though such a path may not be viable for all producers, there is certainly some mileage in the production of consumption sugar. Thus while technically feasible, domestic refining is only an option for a few ACP states on the assumption that they can market their product in the domestic market and export to the immediate region.

Notes

1 COM (81) 68 final, 7 May 1981, pp. 21–23.
2 United Nations World Food Council, 'Food in the Context of the International Development Strategy: A Report by the Executive Director to the Seventh Ministerial Session', Rome, WFC/1981/3, 24 February 1981. Most of these measures are also included in the FAO Plan of Action for World Food Security of November 1979.
3 Food and Agriculture Organisation of the United Nations (FAO), 'Assessment of the Current World Food Security and Stock Situation, and the Short-Term Outlook', Rome, CFS: 81/2, February 1981.
4 D. Gale Johnson, 'The World Food Situation: Developments During the 1970s and Prospects for the 1980s', in *AEI Studies on Contemporary Economic Problems*, William Fellner, Project Director, Washington DC: American Enterprise Institute, 1980.
5 United Nations World Food Council, 'Briefing Note on a New International Wheat Agreement', Rome, 3 November 1980.
6 FAO, 'Steps Taken to Implement the Plan of Action on World Food Security', Rome, CFS: 81/3, March 1981.
7 Barbara Huddleston, 'Responsiveness of Food Aid to Variable Import Requirements', pp. 287–306 in *Food Security for Developing Countries*, Alberto Valdes (ed.), Boulder: Westview Press, 1981.
8 Percentages are of *direct* food aid, i.e. excluding community-level commitments to intergovernmental and non-governmental organisations. The top eleven excludes Kampuchea which is also excluded from the figure of 37 beneficiaries.
9 COM(80) 239, p.11.
10 Dupriez *et al, Integrated Rural Development Projects carried out in Black Africa with EDF aid: Evaluation and Outlook for the future.* Development Series No. 1, Brussels, December 1978.
11 *Community Policy for the North-South Dialogue*, COM(81) 68 final, p. 23.
12 *Proposal for a Council Regulation (EEC) on the Common Organisation of the Market in Sugars* COM(80) 553 final, 30 September 1980
13 House of Lords Select Committee on the European Communities *EEC Sugar Policy* London, HMSO March 19, 1980.
14 House of Lords Select Committee on the European Communities op. cit.

3

Reform of the Common Agricultural Policy and the Third World

Joan Pearce

At the end of June 1981 the EEC Commission presented to the Council of Ministers a major report on reforming the Community's budget, which included proposals for changing the Common Agricultural Policy (CAP). A substantive Council response to this document was not immediately forthcoming, both because of the political importance of the proposals and because of the change in government in France. A response is expected in Autumn 1981, but the process of agreeing upon precise reforms and implementing them is likely to stretch into 1982 and beyond. The debate among the Ten is being conducted almost exclusively in terms of internal EEC considerations, yet some of the changes being proposed have major implications for the Third World. The Commission report of June 1981 is an imprecise document which lists a range of possible changes which would affect the Third World in different ways and to different degrees. There are substantial differences of opinion within and among the member states on which proposals should be adopted. The coming months will see, therefore, a continuing debate which, while conducted largely in internal EEC terms, may have great significance for both agricultural exporting and importing countries in the Third World. Those who are concerned to safeguard Third World interests should follow this debate and attempt to influence it. This chapter aims to provide them with the necessary background information on attitudes towards and criticisms of the CAP in the member states, on the Commission's initial proposals and their possible implications for the Third World, and on the likely reaction of the Ten to these proposals.

Origins and evolution of the CAP

When the European Community was created the six member states agreed to aim first to achieve economic union, which was to embrace trade in agricultural as well as industrial products. The Treaty of Rome set five objectives for agricultural policy: increased productivity of agriculture; a fair standard of living for the farm population; stable markets; security of supplies; and reasonable prices for consumers. One reason why the CAP is currently controversial is that these five objectives have not been pursued with the same degree of success.

It was decided to protect agriculture both as a means of achieving these objectives and because the existing agricultural policies of the member states were for the most part highly protectionist. The Common Agricultural Policy (CAP) that emerged embodied three major components: markets and prices; external relations; and structure. Just as the fulfilment of the five objectives of agricultural policy has been uneven, so these three components have, in practice, been accorded different weights. The markets and prices element has proved to be by far the most important, and the three principles on which this part of the policy is based are habitually referred to as the three principles of the CAP. They are: *a unified market*, implying common prices, which was to enable free circulation of goods; *Community preference*, which was to protect the unified market from imports and fluctuations in world markets by subjecting imports to levies that would ensure they could not undercut Community prices; and *financial solidarity*, which was to allocate the function of channelling the financing of the policy to a Community institution (the European Agricultural Guidance and Guarantee Fund, FEOGA).

External relations have played a much smaller role in the CAP than markets and prices. Article 110 of the Treaty of Rome, which applies to agricultural and non-agricultural trade, stipulates that the member states intend to contribute to the smooth development of world trade, the progressive elimination of international trade restrictions and the lowering of tariff barriers. The Community claims that this undertaking has been fulfilled through bilateral agreements with the EFTA states and some countries in Latin America and the Mediterranean; participation in the GATT multilateral trade negotiations; the generalised system of preferences (see Chapter 5); and special arrangements with the ACP countries (see *Survey 1*, Chapter 3) and New Zealand. Considerations relating to these commitments, however, have been subordinated to the price policy, which requires the Community to be insulated from the world market.

Structural policy has similarly been of secondary significance. The objectives set in the Treaty of Rome require that agriculture attain a satisfactory level of economic efficiency. During the 1960s efforts were concentrated on establishing common prices, and not until 1972 were any common structural measures adopted. These concerned modernisation of farms, encouragement of small farmers to cease production and the organisation of farms in larger units, and assistance for training in agricultural skills. A subsequent measure was aimed specifically at mountain and hill areas and other less-favoured areas, while another provided aid for marketing and processing projects. In the short run, however, it was more effective and cheaper to use price-policy to maintain an adequate level of farm income than to use structural policy to help farmers either to improve their earning power in agriculture or to move out of agriculture. In the longer run, a more energetic structural policy could have made agriculture more efficient so that a lower level of prices could have ensured the same level of farm incomes.

The centrality of the price mechanism and the way in which it evolved have prompted various criticisms. Prices were intended to serve the dual role of maintaining farm incomes and securing balance between Community supply and demand. When common prices were established throughout the Community they were set at a high level on the insistence of West Germany, which did not wish to lower its prices by the full amount needed to conform with those of other countries. At the same time for a large part of production intervention agencies were set up, which effectively ensured that farmers could sell at a guaranteed price all that they produced. The high price level and guaranteed prices, together with improved productivity, encouraged production to rise, causing the Community to reach and then exceed self-sufficiency in some products, notably dairy products, sugar and cereals.

As long as the Community was a net importer of most products, securing market balance could be seen as synonymous with attaining self-sufficiency, and hence with the objective of security of supply. As surpluses developed, raising prices no longer served to secure market balance but the political and social arguments for maintaining farm incomes predominated. Because prices were not curbed, surpluses continued to grow and became an increasing burden on the Community budget, from which the cost of disposing of them has to be covered through paying for storage, for destruction, or for export restitutions to producers who sell to third countries at prices below those prevailing in the Community.

Criticisms of the CAP

A basic criticism of the CAP is that, since it entails production of goods for which there is no market (at the price set by the Community), it would be more efficient to allocate to another sector the resources used to produce these goods. It is further suggested that because the intervention system guarantees a minimum price for all production there has been inadequate price competition within the Community, so that the division of labour in accordance with comparative advantage which should have resulted from the establishment of free trade among the member states has only partially materialised.

Critics also point out that the CAP has created or exacerbated imbalances within the Community. Although the maintenance of farm income is the prime rationale for steadily raising prices, the divergence in farm incomes has increased with some farmers barely able to scrape a living while others are comfortably off. This has arisen partly from the ability of large-scale farmers to take greater advantage than smaller farmers of the opportunities afforded by the CAP, and partly from the fact that the CAP provides a much larger measure of support for some products than for others. The differentiated treatment of products similarly results in imbalances among member states, since certain types of production are concentrated in certain countries, notably Mediterranean products in Italy. Imbalances have also been generated by the transfer of resources from consumers (who include food-processing industries and livestock rearers as well as households) to producers which the high level of Community food prices entails, and from taxpayers to farmers as a result of surpluses. These transfers are reflected at the national level in the form of trade flows and of financial flows through the budget from member states that are net importers of agricultural products to those that are net exporters.

Fault is found too with the system of external protection operated by the CAP. Food exporters (both in the Third World and among developed countries) have complained that it reduces export outlets for third world countries, depresses world prices and destabilises world markets. Furthermore, these effects have been exacerbated by the growth of surpluses, which have caused the Community's import demand to dwindle and its efforts to compete in world markets to increase. Food importers (including those in the Third World) benefit from lower world prices, but also suffer from instability in world markets. Besides being undesirable in themselves these adverse repercussions on the rest of the world are deemed to impinge on the Community's exports of non-agricultural goods and generally to detract from its international image.

Budget pressures for reform

Whereas these shortcomings have not carried enough weight with member states to convince them that the CAP should be reformed, pressure has now built up from the budget which will necessitate change of some sort in the CAP. One factor is the British budget problem which lies in the fact that despite being one of the poorer members of the Community, Britain was by 1980 the largest net contributor to the budget. This happened chiefly because Britain is a large importer of agricultural products and consequently benefits comparatively little from agricultural expenditure, which accounts for the lion's share of the budget. For Britain's contribution to be noticeably reduced by restructuring the budget, the proportion spent on agriculture would have to be cut back sizably.

A second source of pressure is the increase in total budget expenditure. Revenue is made up of agricultural levies, customs duties and up to 1 % of the value added tax base of member states. For several years expenditure was well within this limit but as it rose it took up an increasing proportion of the value added tax and began to approach the ceiling of 1 %. The nearing of the ceiling demonstrates that the financial arrangements of the CAP were devised for a situation where products were in deficit and are much less suited to dealing with surpluses. As the Community has moved from being a net importer to being a net exporter of some products, revenue from import levies has declined relative to expenditure on disposing of surpluses.

Expenditure in excess of the ceiling will undoubtedly be necessitated when Spain and Portugal join the Community. Once the number of Mediterranean member states is increased there will also be growing pressure for the CAP to treat southern products in the same way as northern products. This could mean either extending the amount of support given to southern products or curbing that for northern products.

Spending on the CAP is therefore being squeezed from three directions:

- moves, associated with restructuring, to increase expenditure on other policies;
- a threatened shortage of revenue when the own resources ceiling is reached;
- and the expectation that some additional expenditure will be unavoidable once Spain and Portugal become member states.

In response to these pressures the Commission and other interested parties have prepared proposals for changing the CAP. Because it is pressure on the budget that has prompted active consideration of possible revisions to the CAP, the proposals are generally conceived in the context of relieving that pressure. Some of the suggested ways of doing this would leave the CAP operating essentially as at present and would have little effect on its overall cost; these would mean shifting the costs of the CAP from the Community budget to consumers or to national budgets, or to third countries including ldcs. Other proposals would imply more radical reform to reduce both budget and non-budget costs.

Raising more revenue

Broadly speaking there are three approaches to tackling the problem of the budget: to raise budget revenue, to curb budget expenditure, or in some way to bypass the existing budget arrangements. The most straightforward way to increase budget revenue would be to raise the 1 % VAT ceiling on own resources. All governments acknowledge, though not necessarily in their public utterances, that the own resources will eventually have to be expanded. Several of them, however, are for the time being firmly opposed to this. Part of the explanation is that in the current climate of recession their national public finances are meeting with difficulty. Some member states insist that before agreeing to an increase in revenue they want to see more balanced expenditure among the various policies (and hence among member states). Others would like first to see the discipline of the own resources ceiling effect a tightening up of the operation of the CAP that would leave it more efficient and less open to criticism.

The bulk of opinion among member states is for the time being against raising the own resources ceiling, a step which would moreover require the approval of national parliaments. At present it is advanced less as an immediate policy proposal than as something that should be kept on the agenda. However, one measure that would be an additional source of budget revenue and would not breach the 1% ceiling is the imposition of import duties. There is vigorous support in some quarters for the imposition of duties on products that are imported for use as animal feedstuff compounds, which could affect some ldcs significantly. These compounds consist of protein, usually provided by oilseeds such as soya, and cereals or cereal substitutes. Most of the oilseeds are imported, as are cereal substitutes, which include manioc (tapioca), offals, maize gluten, citrus residues and many other things. It is argued that to tax these imports more heavily would not only generate increased revenue but would also reduce surpluses. Surpluses of cereals would be reduced because substitutes would be more costly so the demand for cereals would rise, and surpluses of dairy products would also fall because the higher cost of inputs would deter some dairy production and, moreover, the higher cost of soya meal would encourage pig producers to switch to using skimmed milk for feed, while the higher cost of soya and other edible oils would raise the price of margarine and so increase demand for butter.

Whereas the Community imports soya chiefly from the United States, it imports other oilseeds and manioc from Third World countries. In the case of manioc, raising the levy above 6% would contravene a GATT ruling, and the Commission has instead secured agreement from Thailand to restrict imports to about 5m tons a year, against a peak of 6m in 1978. Any further reduction would be strongly resisted by West Germany and the Netherlands, which are large importers of manioc.

Curbing expenditure

Proposals for curbing expenditure are directed either towards effecting savings on the way in which the CAP operates, or towards lowering surplus production through quantitative restrictions or a restrictive price policy. Various ways are suggested of reducing the CAP's running costs without modifying any of its essential features, though some of them would affect the Third World. The intervention system could be managed more astutely, quality controls applied more rigorously (incidentally benefiting consumers), some of the special subsidies and premiums reduced or removed, and export policy formulated more coherently. This last would include steadier supplies to world markets, long-term supply agreements, a well-conceived food aid policy and collaboration with other exporting countries in organising world markets, in particular to hold world prices closer to Community prices. Egypt, Algeria and some Lomé countries would welcome long-term supply contracts with the Community, though some of the Community's major competitors in world agricultural markets have described them as 'institutionalised dumping'.

There are several difficulties with following this option. It is not clear that the savings effected would be adequate to do more than stave off the time when more far-reaching measures would have to be applied. On the other hand, those who wish the CAP to be revised radically would not be satisfied. Further, some of the savings would entail costs to some member states and not others, for example, quality control or the disappearance of particular subsidies and premiums.

Quantitative restrictions can take a variety of forms, and already exist for sugar in the form of a quota system. Their basic characteristic is that they limit the amount that can be sold at the guaranteed price and so deter farmers from producing quantities above that limit. If applied they would probably have a more direct impact on surpluses than would other measures, but they are difficult to negotiate and administer, and have some adverse effects. The negotiating problems arise in the distribution of the quantities among countries and among farms which tends to result in the initial level being set too high. A corollary of this is that imports from Third World countries tend to be squeezed out (as the section on sugar in Chapter 2 shows). Administration is complicated, in varying degrees according to the country and the product, by the need to collect large amounts of information and to maintain extensive control over marketing. Unless there is provision for transferring them, quantitative restrictions freeze the existing structure of production, reduce competitiveness and impede increases in productivity. In so far as quantitative restrictions curb budget costs they may reduce pressure for price restraint and so do nothing to alter the transfer of resources from consumers to producers or from net importing countries to net exporting countries. There is too a risk of production from net exporters being dumped on net importers and of trade barriers being set up in retaliation.

A restrictive price policy could be implemented by agreement at the annual price fixing either to freeze prices or sharply to curtail increases. Because price curbs would squeeze farmers' incomes, proposals for them are often coupled with schemes of direct income support or of structural measures that would enable farmers to modernise or adapt their farms or to go out of production.

One way of effectively bypassing the budget would be for national governments to take on part of the expenditure. Another is for the Community to obtain from producers some financial contribution to the cost of disposing of surpluses. This has already been done in the dairy and sugar sectors by applying a general co-responsibility levy amounting to 2 % of producers' revenue. One more possibility is to devise a budget mechanism that would redistribute member states' net contributions.

In addition, there have been pressures to effect an apparent cut in agricultural spending by transferring items of expenditure to other budget heads. It is argued that the proportion of the budget spent on agriculture is exaggerated because items are assigned to the CAP that should appear under different headings. Assistance to ldcs has been a particular focus for attention – for example, food aid, sugar arrangements with developing countries, and preferential trading agreements – although monetary compensatory amounts have also been mentioned. The one specific attempt to shift expenditure from one budget head to another involved the Third World. The Commission proposed in 1977 that the cost of the ACP sugar arrangement should be classified as development and not as agricultural expenditure. This attempt failed but it gave rise to fears that if sugar (or indeed that part of food aid at present included in the agricultural budget) were transferred to development, the aid expenditure category would show an increase and attempts would be made to offset it by reducing more conventional aid.

Approaches of member states

France

The government of M. Giscard d'Estaing refrained from presenting a detailed formulation of its position on changing the CAP before the presidential election for fear that this might adversely affect the farm vote. Since M. Mitterrand was elected, efforts to define an agricultural policy have concentrated on the national level, and a precise statement on policy towards changing the CAP is likely to be presented in Autumn 1981.

The basis of the new government's approach to agriculture is quite distinct from that of its predecessor. Under M. Giscard d'Estaing the concept was developed of agriculture as France's 'green petrol', a reference both to the wealth, particularly export earnings, that it was intended to generate and to its potential role as a strategic resource. Structural policy assisted small farmers to leave the land and facilitated concentration of farms. The Socialist government also aims to increase agricultural production and productivity but lays much more stress on the distribution of income within the sector; similarly, it also aims to expand exports, but is concerned that those which go as food aid to the Third World should better match the needs of the recipient countries. Its structural policy seems likely to be oriented to stemming the decline in the rural population by installing a new generation of younger farmers.

Some aspects of the new policy will not be easily inserted into the European framework, and as yet there is scant indication of how the Mitterrand government would set about doing this. Although it may now revise the previous French position that the 1 % ceiling should not be exceeded, ways of curbing expenditure will still need to be found. Like its predecessor, this government will probably opt for quantitative restrictions with the difference that it will include an element of progressivity, that is, larger farmers receiving guaranteed prices for a smaller proportion of their production than small farmers. It has already begun to press for action on imported cereal substitutes, which would benefit small-scale French dairy farmers at the expense of large-scale farmers in the Netherlands and elsewhere, though the argument used is that unless farmers are given guarantees on Community preference they cannot be asked to take on the financial burden implicit in budget restraint. In the broader European context the new French government may seek to extend the scope of cooperation with other member states and be more receptive to their concerns.

West Germany

The most recent statements on Germany's position on the CAP list four objectives: the VAT ceiling of 1 % must not be exceeded; spending on agriculture must rise more slowly than own resources; market forces must be brought to bear more and producers made to assume more responsibility for marketing their products; and resort should not be had to tougher import restrictions and aggressive export promotion. To avoid unacceptable hardship to low income farmers, direct income aids could be provided as a social measure to be nationally financed. Financial management should also be improved: decisions of the Council of Ministers and the Commission must not entail exceeding the appropriations for the year. It is observed that budget restructuring cannot be realised solely by correcting the CAP.

This last point reflects Germany's overriding concern with budgetary aspects of the CAP. Negotiations about Britain's budget contribution highlighted the fact that Germany made a very large net contribution to the Community budget, and resulted in Germany footing the bulk of the bill for Britain's budget rebates. Particularly in view of the present straitened circumstances of its public finances, Germany is anxious for a reduction in its budget contribution. Hence Germany emphasises, in the context of the CAP, the necessity of keeping within the 1 % ceiling and of effecting a relative decline in spending on agriculture, and the need for an automatic mechanism either within or outside the budget that would enable a redistribution of member states' contributions. What form such a mechanism would take has yet to be defined, though Helmut Schmidt has several times referred to the setting of ceilings for contributions. Although the German government is in principle in favour of reforming the CAP, its approach is distinctly gradualist, reflecting the objections of German farmers and the reluctance of its own Minister of Agriculture. By contrast, the desire to alleviate its financial burden is very urgent. Consequently it supports co-responsibility in the dairy sector, and might be persuaded to accept some form of quantitative restriction, despite several reservations.

Italy

Italy incurs large resource costs as a result of the CAP, reflecting the fact that it is an exporter of Mediterranean products but a large net importer of northern agricultural products, which are much more favoured by the CAP. The benefits that the CAP does confer on Italy, for both its northern and its southern products derive more from schemes specifically designed for Italy than from the basic system. In pressing for more support from the Community for its agriculture Italy stresses the need for structural measures and for the development of non-agricultural policies, namely social and regional policies. Much concern is voiced about the prospects for Italy's Mediterranean products when the Community is enlarged and warnings are sounded that unless greater support is given to these products a 'war among the poor' may ensue. Since extending structural and other measures and assisting Mediterranean agriculture would entail higher expenditure, an increase in the own resources ceiling above 1% of VAT is often advocated.

Increasing disparity between farm incomes in the North and South of the country has led the Italian government to press for a reform of the CAP that would ensure that Mediterranean products enjoyed as much support as northern products. There has been some discussion of reducing surpluses by means of a system of quotas with differential prices. This has yet to be adopted as government policy and may not be because of the difficulty of finding some way of defending deficit countries from dumping by surplus countries. Italy also accepts the general co-responsibility levy but would expect to be exempted from any extension of the super-levy because it is far from self-sufficient in dairy products.

Britain

The British government's chief objective in negotiations on the budget and the CAP will be to find something more than a temporary means of reducing the size of its net budget contribution. Consequently it will oppose an increase in the own resources ceiling and will seek ways of curbing expenditure on the CAP. It does not, however, believe that whatever reforms are agreed for the CAP they will alone be sufficient quickly to correct those aspects of the budget that it considers unfair. The British view is that the budget fails to ensure that resources tend to flow from prosperous to less prosperous member states, and that a mechanism should be introduced to correct this shortcoming.

The three principles that the British Chancellor of the Exchequer has advanced as a basis for CAP reform are a reduction in the support for products in surplus, notably milk and cereals; freer play for market forces; and tight control of spending on all support. Britain is attracted by options that would shift part of the financing of the CAP to national exchequers, either by combining price restrictions with nationally financed direct income aids to compensate small farmers or by making national governments directly responsible for a certain percentage of the cost of price support. Quantitative restrictions are regarded less favourably, but not ruled out. What would be resisted would be the introduction of an element of progressivity since this would militate against British farmers who are organised in larger units than most continental farmers.

The fact that the negotiations are taking place during Britain's presidency puts it at a disadvantage. First, it is difficult from the Chair to argue forcefully in the face of opposition. Second, Britain will be anxious if not to complete the negotiations at least to have the basic outline of an agreement by the end of its term. To achieve little or no progress would reflect badly on British diplomacy at a time when the Foreign Office is keen to take a lead in other aspects of the Community, particularly political cooperation. This effectively rules out for Britain the tactic of allowing things to drag on to the point where the own resources were exhausted and there had to be resort to a measure of national financing.

Denmark

Denmark is keenly aware of its economy's dependence on agricultural exports. Great importance is attached to maintaining the three principles of the CAP, since it is believed that to relax any one of them would be to threaten the free circulation of goods within the Community. The CAP is sufficiently important that the Danish government would be prepared to raise the own resources limit but is not currently advancing this proposal because it is aware of the opposition in other member states. In present economic circumstances such a move would also be politically unpopular within Denmark, and the government also appreciates that the budget constraint could be used to remove some of the least rational elements of the CAP.

To curb expenditure Denmark advocates in the short term adjusting the CAP mechanisms and in the long term expanding exports. Short-term adjustments include abolishing some schemes oriented towards incomes and restoring to intervention agencies their intended role as a safety net by such means as tightening quality control. In making these adjustments the criterion should be whether they bring the operation of the CAP closer to the market mechanism, not the costs and benefits to particular member states, though attempts should be made to distribute sacrifices fairly. Efforts to cope with surpluses, particularly of dairy products should be intensified. The general co-responsibility levy should be used to influence production, not just as a source of finance, and there should be no broad exemptions from the super-levy. In the longer run exports to third countries should be developed, helped by rising world prices. Export policy should not be aggressive but based on cooperation with other exporters of agricultural products.

To help farmers suffering hardship, structural policy should be expanded, preferably in the direction of persuading them to switch into a different type of production rather than to leave the land. Direct income aids might have to be used in some cases, but should be avoided because they are costly and tend to encourage farmers to continue producing inefficiently.

Ireland

Ideally Ireland would like to see the own resources limit raised but acknowledges that for the time being this is not a practicable possibility. In the context of alternative approaches Ireland usually claims it should be treated as a special case because its economy is very highly dependent on agriculture, its agriculture sector is far from attaining the limits of its productive capacity and it has a low level of per capita GNP. Ireland would support quantitative restrictions in the Community only if it was largely exempt from them, though it might be willing to concede a degree of price restraint in return. It favours taxing imported cereal substitutes because this would increase the contributions of those member states where substitutes were used while improving the competitive position of Irish dairy farmers, who rely on pasture. Ireland is totally opposed to national financing because it does not have the resources to match what other member states could offer their producers and because it believes this would be the thin end of the wedge leading to the collapse of the CAP.

Netherlands

For the immediate future the Netherlands would like to see the 1% VAT ceiling maintained, not for its own sake but so as to prompt a rationalisation of the CAP. Emphasis is placed on the need to maintain the free flow of trade both within the Community and between the Community and the rest of the world, and a clear distinction made between the financial aspects and the trade aspects of the CAP. It is suggested that if the Community does not have enough funds to support a fully fledged CAP it should at least ensure that expenditure is organised in a way that would guarantee free trade. Consequently the Netherlands favours adjusting some mechanisms and tightening the intervention system, but is opposed to national financing, unless it is operated at the Community level, because it would segment the market. It also objects to quantitative restrictions, though might reluctantly accept them.

The need for action on surpluses is acknowledged with the proviso that the burden should be shared. The Netherlands is not prepared to curb its dairy production just so that other member states can expand theirs. Hence it accepts the general co-responsibility levy, and also the super-levy if there are few or no exemptions. There are, however, doubts as to whether co-responsibility levies alone could have an adequate impact on either finance or production. The Netherlands will resist French pressure for severely curtailing imports of cereal substitutes.

The Commission's proposals

At the end of June 1981 the Commission presented a report on the Mandate it had been given a year earlier to examine the development of Community policies with a view to proposing structural changes in the budget that would prevent the recurrence of 'unacceptable situations' like that created by the British budget contribution. The Commission report endeavours to set the Mandate within a broad framework. The opening paragraphs speak of the duty to defend and develop the shared inheritance that already exists by devising a joint strategy for tackling the economic problems besetting the Community. The report then commends the evolution of the single internal market for industrial goods and the common agricultural policy but acknowledges that other policies have not advanced at the same pace and that changes in the international economy have generated new requirements. There follows a shopping list of the areas in which the Community needs to progress. Closer coordination is needed of member states' monetary and economic policies, which would be greatly facilitated by expansion of the European Monetary System. The customs union should be completed by eliminating the various trade barriers that still remain. A new strategy is required for energy and for advanced technology, and an active competition policy is essential.

After setting out this list, however, the report avers that 'it is hard to see how the Community can hope to advance in a balanced, decisive fashion on these various points unless it puts its budgetary affairs in order'. The Commission's proposals, it continues, concern essentially the common agricultural policy, regional policy and social policy, and 'The major effort concerns the common agricultural policy'. The CAP is thus placed firmly in the context of budgetary problems. Despite an earlier assertion that Community policies have economic implications far transcending the budget, scant attention is paid to the non-budget effects of the CAP, and all references to costs relate only to budget costs.

Not only is the CAP dealt with solely in a budgetary context, but even within the confines of the budget no major shift is envisaged. The Commission sets its guidelines for the CAP with the modest aim of ensuring that spending on it grows less rapidly than do own resources. For some years the proportion of the budget devoted to the CAP will remain large and a special mechanism involving sizable refunds will be needed if the United Kingdom's contribution to the budget is to be reduced.

The Commission sets out seven guidelines for future decisions on the CAP.

1. and 2. *Price policy and export policy* are highly interdependent in the context of the Commission's recommendation that the Community should aim gradually to align guaranteed prices with prices ruling on a better organised world market. This could be achieved by pursuing a rigorous policy towards prices within the Community and adopting a more active export policy designed to stabilise world prices by means of cooperation agreements with other major exporters, possibly supplemented by long-term export contracts.

3. *Production targets* are proposed to make producers more aware of market realities. They should be set for all major products to signify the volume of production that the Community wants to guarantee at the full price. The Commission has indicated that the target level might equate to more or less than self-sufficiency depending on the product. It has yet to specify the criteria that should be applied, but for each product they would take into account trends in production and consumption, the degree of self-sufficiency desired, import commitments, export markets and food aid requirements. Once the target was reached producers would no longer receive the full price. Again the arrangements would vary among products: for sugar, the existing quota system should continue; for cereals, tonnages above the production target should receive a lower intervention price; for dairy products, co-responsibility should be extended, or else, the Commission warns, other measures will be inevitable.

4. *Structural policy* should be tailored to the needs of individual agricultural regions. Measures are to be prepared to assist in resolving the problems of Mediterranean agriculture, and will be presented to the Council and Parliament before the end of 1982. These will be medium-term programmes covering an integrated policy for incomes, markets, production and structures, and involving both financial and agricultural instruments of the Community.

5. *Income support* subsidies are envisaged as a possible supplementary measure in specific circumstances. Since the criteria for granting them would be established by the Community they might be partly financed by the Community; in view of the cost involved they would have to be confined to certain small producers.

6. *Quality control and financial control* should be reinforced. More rigorous quality control would help reduce surpluses by excluding some production from the scope of the market organisations and would also contribute to export promotion. Tighter financial control would mean the Commission regulating the way that Community finance is managed in the member states.

7. *National aids* are to be subjected to greater discipline by the Commission.

Implications for the Third World

It is not possible to establish precisely at this stage the net effect of changes in the CAP on the Third World. This is partly because the final outcome of internal EEC negotiations is, as yet, far from certain. But it is also because the Third World is not a homogeneous group. The effect of the CAP in its present form, and the effect of any changes in it vary according to commodities and, as noted in Chapter 2, according to whether the ldc in question is an importer or exporter. However, while the precise impact on particular countries will only become apparent over time, it is possible to identify those proposed reforms with implications for ldcs to which the Commission attaches high priority and to indicate the type of impact they might have on agricultural exporting and importing states.

The Commission has devised proposals that would leave the principles and mechanisms of the CAP essentially intact while adjusting the mechanisms to ensure that budget expenditure rises less rapidly than do own resources, but leaving the main burden of restructuring the budget, in the immediate future, to a budget mechanism. The assessment that seems to have guided the Commission is that those member states that most want the CAP changed (the United Kingdom and West Germany) are chiefly concerned with its budget implications,[1] whereas those that least want it changed (Benelux, Denmark, Ireland and probably France) are less reluctant to make concessions on budgetary than on other aspects. However, this emphasis on the budget may be combined with two other measures that have implications for the Third World.

The first is to formulate a more coherent and, perhaps, aggressive export policy. Although the report states that a trade strategy of the sort proposed by the Commission 'would not damage the interests of developing countries' there are some grounds for concern. The Commission has indicated that the two guidelines to which it attaches greatest importance are price policy and production targets. Most commentators have interpreted the aim of aligning Community prices with world prices as meaning lower Community prices. In fact, what the Commission appears to have in mind is in the short run to continue the existing policy of trying to keep Community price increases to modest proportions and in the long run to collaborate with other major suppliers to raise the level of world prices.

The effects of production targets will depend on the level at which they are set. The higher they are the easier it will be to agree on them but the less impact they will have on reducing surpluses. If the surpluses are not greatly reduced it will be difficult to increase world prices by much, at least for more than a short time. At best there would be a small decline in surpluses, a small narrowing of the gap between Community and world prices, and hence a small reduction in the cost of surplus disposal. From the point of view of Third World exporters, the higher the production targets the lower is the risk that their access to the Community will be directly affected, although as the case of sugar indicates (see Chapter 2) there may be indirect effects in the medium-term. On the other hand, if production targets are lower there will be more pressure from EEC producers for increases in the Community's prices. The more the Community's prices rise, the more it will need to push up world prices if the gap between them is to be closed. Thus, while low targets would be more successful in cutting the Community's surpluses, their disposal would probably still be as costly. Third World exporters could well find their goods being squeezed out of Community markets as the price of EEC farmers' acceptance of the lower limits, while at the same time facing less severe competition from the Community in other markets. Higher world prices might compensate Third World food exporters for the loss of Community markets, they would certainly be detrimental to the interests of food importers.

The second area concerns improving the treatment of Mediterranean products. At the present time, a number of Third World states, particularly those in the southern Mediterranean, have limited access to the European market for products that might be covered by any such charges in policy. These exports would be put at risk for the reasons explained in *Survey 1* (see Chapter 4) in relation to the impact of EEC enlargement.

The Commission's proposals can be criticised by those who wish for a radical reform of the CAP on the grounds that they provide, at best, palliatives. Critics will say that the Commission should have taken a firm lead, that the longer it goes on accommodating the views of member states the longer they will take to change. The Commission's defence is that for political reasons only gradual progress is feasible. But if progress is too gradual it may be too late. From the viewpoint of the developing countries, the main worry is that during the hard negotiations between the various interests in the EEC it may prove to be politically easier to achieve changes at the expense of third parties. Such changes could include import duties or export subsidies, which would affect primarily Third World agricultural exporters, or they could include efforts to raise world prices, which would affect primarily Third World food importers.

Note

1 The Commission did not admit West Germany's claim that it was in an 'unacceptable situation' with regard to its budget contribution.

Part 2
Industrial Protectionism and the Third World

4

Recent Trends in Industrial Protectionism in the EEC

Geoffrey Shepherd

From tariff to non-tariff protection

The level of tariff protection in industrialised countries has continued to fall in the post-war years as a result of successive tariff cutting rounds and the spread of preferential tariff arrangements. This liberalisation has been offset by an extension of non-tariff import barriers (NTBs) – for instance, quantitative restrictions, technical controls and bureaucratic hindrance – and of subsidies to domestic industries. Many observers argue that, on the whole, this 'new protectionism' has not entirely offset the liberalisation gains in tariff protection, but others see it as a major discouragement to the manufactured exports of developing countries. This section reviews the major recent trends in non-tariff import protectionism in the EEC, as well as the recent evolution of the free-trader protectionist debate in the major member countries.

It is extremely difficult to assemble information on NTBs to imports that is either qualitatively complete or quantitatively assessable.[1] As a result it is difficult to interpret trends: some have argued that our worst fears on protectionism as it affected developing countries in the 1970s were not, or not entirely, realised;[2] this line of argument could imply an optimism for the 1980s which others might find hard to justify in the light of the remarkable growth of anti-Japanese protectionist sentiment in Western Europe and North America in the most recent period. It is easiest to make sense of trends in NTB protection if we define specific categories of problems viz textiles, steel, Japanese electro-mechanical products, US chemicals, and miscellaneous products.

Textiles are the longest-standing trade problem. For the Third World, NTBs in textiles constitute the single most important hindrance to trade in manufactures and are the basis on which, rightly or wrongly, many generalisations about the new protectionism have been made. The major industrialised countries have placed barriers in the way of low-cost imports, mainly from Japan (before the 1970s) and the Newly

Industrialising Countries (NICs), for several decades. With the negotiation in 1977 of the second Multi-Fibre Arrangement (MFA 2) these barriers took on a new restrictiveness, especially in the case of the EEC. It is unlikely that this restrictiveness will be relaxed under MFA 3 and the new bilateral agreements that the EEC will negotiate with individual supplier countries in 1982. The background of the MFA is described in more detail in Chapter 6.

During the 1970s steel tended to constitute the second most important product group where formal NTBs hindered trade, in addition to which subsidies to national industries have loomed large. Until about 1977, these restrictions were almost entirely aimed at Japan (with some US restrictions also on imports from the EEC). But in 1978 the steel exporting NICs were obliged to conclude so-called voluntary export restraints (VERs) with the EEC, though they account for only a small share of EEC imports and are of little consequence in the adjustment problems of its steel industry. Some of these agreements were discontinued however in 1980.

Japan's earliest major export thrusts were met with NTBs as in the case of textiles and steel, or by subsidies to domestic industry (shipbuilding). Japan's export thrust in the 1970s in electro-mechanical industries has been led by cars and colour TVs and is now increasingly turning to more sophisticated items such as advanced machine tools, video-recorders and electronic components. The rapid growth and degree of product concentration in Japanese exports, together with the (not unrelated) development of a considerable and widening bilateral EEC trade deficit with Japan, has resulted in major trade friction and a rapid growth in NTBs. Indeed, while it was the fashion in the aftermath of the first oil crisis (1975–77) to see the NICs as the main source of disruption and the major target for protection, it is clear that in the aftermath of the second oil crisis the EEC's attention has swung dramatically to Japan. A patchwork of unilateral and bilateral 'voluntary' restraints on EEC imports from Japan grew up in the 1970s. For instance the UK negotiated VERs on TVs in 1973 and cars in 1976, while unilateral French restraints were imposed on cars in 1977. However, the most dramatic developments followed the US VER on cars negotiated with Japan in May, 1981. In June, Canada, Germany, Belgium and the Netherlands promptly followed suit with VERs. There is a continuing strong European pressure for Japanese restraint in other items such as colour TV tubes and machine tools, and there is every indication that, as Japan continues to export increasingly sophisticated goods in the 1980s, European (as well as North American) industrialists will continue to press for protection.

The weak US dollar, the more general US competitive strength in mature industries where economies of scale are important, and favourable raw material prices has led to rapid increases in US chemical and synthetic textile (yarns, carpets) exports in recent years. This in turn has created problems for the EEC chemical and textile industries, which were already suffering from recession and over-capacity. In 1980 the UK was able to persuade the EEC to impose temporary quotas on imports of some synthetic yarns from the USA, although with the mid-1981 revaluation of the dollar, much of the steam has gone out of this particular issue for the moment at least.

The member countries of the EEC, as well as the EEC as a group in some cases, continue to maintain formal NTBs on a variety of extra-EEC imports. These include NTBs by the EEC on paper products from EFTA countries, by the UK on non-leather footwear, jute and polypropylene products, aimed mainly at NICs, by France on enamelware from Spain, and by Italy on some consumer electronic items. In all, these miscellaneous restrictions are not aimed systematically at the developing world, account for relatively little of total trade, and cannot be said to show any clear tendency to grow. A potentially more worrying phenomenon is the existence and possible growth of intra-EEC trade frictions. These are most evident in textiles, for instance French imports of Italian knitwear and the more general problem of the free circulation within the Community of imports that have been outward processed, but they are also nascent in areas such as consumer electronics and cars where some European manufacturers are beginning to use increasing amounts of imported Japanese components.

Protectionist pressures in EEC states

In spite of some common trends, important differences in attitudes to protection have emerged among EEC countries. With a strong original post-war commitment to free trade, the *UK* has undergone a considerable conversion during the 1970s to the point where it has become potentially the most protectionist Community member. Protectionist sentiment has generally been fuelled by the economy's poor growth record in the 1970s, an unemployment situation that is critical, the particular effects on competitiveness of the high value of the pound in recent years, and a general pessimism about the economy's adaptability to changing international conditions of competition. The case for selective import controls on the grounds that the economy's growth is constrained by a structurally weak balance of payments has been urged by the Cambridge School of economists. This doctrine, which argues the case for selective controls against high-technology (i.e. advanced-country) rather than against low-technology (i.e. developing country) imports, has influenced the thinking of the Left, to the point where selective import controls and withdrawal from the EEC customs union have become part of the policy proposals of the Labour Party, since it has been in opposition, and of the Trades Union Congress. The case for import controls has also had some influence on the thinking of the Confederation of British Industry. In spite of a strongly *laissez-faire* philosophy since its accession to power in 1979, the Conservative government has not been able to withstand all the pressures exerted on it for protection (or, for that matter, for subsidies). In spite of warnings to the textile industry that it could not expect featherbedding in the long term, the government has come to push the industry's interests in Brussels, just as strongly as did its Labour predecessor, albeit a little less openly. The UK government has also taken a leading role in demanding restraint from Japanese exporters, and particularly in this context has championed the case for selective safeguards.

Of the larger member states, *Germany* still clearly retains the strongest commitment to free trade. Its 'succumbing' to a VER with Japan on cars in June 1981 was virtually inevitable after the conclusion of the USA VER which left Canada, Germany and the Benelux countries as the only major unprotected national markets in the world. Even so, this move was not taken without much soul-searching, and the German VER has higher growth provisions than do the other Western European and North American limitations on Japanese car imports. Germany, along with the Netherlands and Denmark, is taking a relatively liberal stance on the MFA 3 negotiation, as it did over MFA 2. Nonetheless, in spite of this relative liberalism, Germany *does* protect and there is more than a suspicion that the Federal Government is able to engage in the rhetoric of free trade knowing that the Commission and the other member states will be pursuing a more protectionist line and that Germany's own regional (Land) governments are often willing to come to the aid of 'lame ducks'. The 1970s have seen some signs of a retreat from the consensus politics on stability and growth as ends and on the market mechanism as means, on which the earlier German *Wirtschaftswunder* was partly based. Even though alternative philosophical formulations are a long way from capturing the mainstream of the unions, the political parties (though the SPD is substantially split), or the civil service, protectionist sentiment has clearly begun to spread beyond the traditionally declining sectors (notably textiles) to sectors such as cars. This is partly the result of a somewhat sudden realisation of the extent of the Japanese challenge to Germany's traditional dominance in the electro-mechanical industries. If it is indeed true, as some are beginning to believe, that Germany will progressively lose its technological leadership to Japan (and even to France), the pressures for protection in Germany are likely to grow.

In contradiction to the Anglo-Saxon economic notions that shaped the post-war Western trading system (and which were eagerly espoused by the new post-war Germany), the *French* tradition has been to emphasise the role of state guidance in the industrial growth process and to regard free trade as at best a necessary evil. The notion of 'organised free trade' that has been emphasised in official thinking in the 1970s is one in which both ailing sectors and infant industries may be judiciously protected, not only from imports but also, in some cases, from inward foreign investment. Moreover, the French have been less inhibited than have the

USA, UK, Netherlands and Germany, operating in a more 'Anglo-Saxon' tradition, by what is called in the jargon the principles of transparency. French informal bureaucratic controls on imports, for instance, have some notoriety. Even the liberalisation reforms of the Barre government from 1976 onwards had more effect on price controls and on support to 'lame ducks' than they did on import regimes. France is fertile territory for a hardening of protectionist attitudes which are already prevalent: selective import controls are widely favoured by elements in all the major political parties, by much of the public, and by large parts of industry. In the immediate aftermath of the presidential and parliamentary elections the economic orientation of the new Socialist government is not yet fully clear, but the indications so far are that while the emphasis may well shift more strongly to helping ailing industrial sectors, the government will not have a significantly different approach from its predecessor towards maintaining the international trading system. Like the UK, the French position appears to remain as hard on MFA 3 as it was on MFA 2. At the same time, and unlike the UK, it is possible to detect the growth of some pressures to move France more towards the German position: the emergence of a core of strong clothing firms wishing to profit, as many German firms have done, from outward-processing arrangements is one such pressure. The relationship of outward-processing to the MFA is explained in Chapter 7.

In protectionism, as in other spheres of economic life, labels are more difficult to stick on *Italy* than on other EEC member states. Like Germany, Italy has had a strong commitment to free trade since the Second World War, reflecting its reliance on open export markets. At the same time, the existence of long-standing preemptive controls that have kept Japanese imports at minimal levels, and of various bureaucratic hindrances to trade suggests an import regime resembling that of France. Continuous support for a free trade posture does however appear to be more broadly based than in France, and even extends to Communist trades unions. Advocates of selective import controls exist, but as a minority movement within the Left. In some ways the massive financial support that was offered to ailing large firms in many sectors in the 1970s (notably to chemicals, steel, and textiles) can be seen as the partial result of a desire to avoid the introduction of more direct means of protection. Moreover the generally inefficient domestic distribution system has tended to discriminate against imports, and, therefore, to act as covert protection. In textiles and clothing Italy, like Germany, has reaped substantial benefits from European protectionism because Italian and German exports have been stimulated to fill the gaps left in the markets of other member states. But the importance of protection as a means of safeguarding the domestic Italian market in the 1970s has been less clear. The textile and clothing industry has generally proved to be competitive. However, as Italian industry becomes increasingly uncomfortable about its ability to stay competitive, there are signs that Italy is taking an increasingly protectionist stand, particularly in the MFA 3 preparations, although it is still not at British or French levels. This trend is partly the result of the forging of a new alliance between the textile employers' organisations, especially those representing larger firms, and the unions. This alliance, which is somewhat exceptional in Italy, appears to have been able not only to dictate a harder government line in textile protection, but also to have had the textile sector declared a key sector (under Law 675) eligible for substantial public aid. Some commentators have pointed out how Italy, in contrast to Germany and France, has been developing a comparative advantage in the kind of maturer products where the NICs are strongest, such as shoes, textiles, and some engineering products. To this extent, it is conceivable that Italy's interests may be increasingly in European-wide systems of protection that safeguard its own export markets inside the EEC.

The continuing strong commitment to free trade of all the major political elements in the *Netherlands* no doubt reflects public perceptions of the constraints facing small, open economies. It is striking that during the 1981 elections none of the major political parties made any attempt to challenge the objective of a further liberalisation of world trade. According to one study[3] total effective tariff protection for 17 industrial sectors fell from 8 % in 1970 to 3.8 % in 1977. Even so, effective protection for vulnerable sectors is much higher than this average. Moreover there are some signs of pressure from the government to slow down the rate of liberalisation in certain sectors on the grounds that disruption from industrial adjustment should be minimised, and in order to retain a strategic minimum level of industry in some sectors. In addition, subsidies are concentrated on clothing, textiles, shipping, food and beverages and steel, thus increasing the level of protection against import competition. On NTBs the Dutch record has been good until now except in the case of textiles and, most recently, cars. However, there have been proposals in 1981 for new government procurement policies which may discriminate against foreign suppliers, particularly for high technology goods.

Philosophically, *Belgium* is significantly more inclined to protectionism than is the Netherlands. It has been in the wings supporting the EEC's more protectionist initiatives and has been generous in the subsidies it has given to its domestic industries. In spite of this the protectionism issue does not loom large in Belgian politics.

In *Denmark* industrial subsidies are limited. There is no government ownership of industry and only one case of an industrial producer kept alive by government subsidies, the Danish steel works, although Danish shipyards could not have survived without subsidised interest rates to internationally competitive levels. It is a remarkable feature of Danish society, that, in spite of political pressures from trades unions and certain companies, socialist governments have refrained from trying to maintain employment through loans or grants to companies which have lost their ability to compete on world markets. One reason is that most Danish companies are so small that closures have not been politically unacceptable. Moreover, the Danish economy, like that of the Netherlands, is dependent on export markets, so that it would be beyond the fiscal strength of government to try to sustain production of goods for which there was no market abroad.

Because of high wage levels, Danish companies have specialised in products with a relatively sophisticated technology and limited world markets. They have therefore tended to avoid direct competition with developing country exports which are therefore viewed more as a benefit to consumers than as a threat to Danish production. Moreover, many Danish producers who have found themselves unable to compete with cheaper imports have adopted the strategy of importing competitive products themselves and marketing them along with domestic products. They therefore stand to lose rather than gain by restrictions on imports and therefore do not advocate policies of protection. Hence there is not a very strongly articulated domestic opposition to the liberal influence exerted by the Danish government on EEC trade policies for textiles, footwear and leather. Outside the context of the MFA, no Danish unilateral restrictions are enforced on imports from developing countries, and only a small number of products from state trading countries remain subject to quantitative import regulations.

The Treaty of Rome provided for a common commercial policy of its signatory states and gave the Community institutions the responsibility for formulating this. If, in this brief review, the member states have loomed larger than the EEC itself, this reflects the extent to which NTB protection is nationally based. Even textile protection under the MFA consists of *national* quotas that are Community-administered. It is difficult to say what role the Commission as such has played and whether the outcome of member state bargaining in textile and steel protection has led to solutions that are, in aggregate, more protective than they would otherwise have been if they had been purely national. It is tempting to argue that, in textiles at least, the existence of the EEC has been a force for relative liberalism if only because the outcome has had greater transparency in methods of protection (in spite of the arcana of the EEC's system of protection!), as well as a certain pressure on the least liberal importers to import more. Much to the Commission's chagrin, the response to the problem of Japanese imports has so far occurred mainly on a bilateral basis. Pressure is likely to grow for a harmonisation or integration of member state policies, if only because bilateralism threatens the very existence of the customs union.

This brief survey suggests that in one member state, the UK, the portents for protection are ominous, and that they are worrying in the other large member states. It is true that as far as developing country manufactured exports were concerned, trends in protectionism had become worrying a decade ago, even before the onset of worldwide recession, and that the worst fears then have not been realised. This could be construed as a basis for optimism concerning the immediate future, particularly since the emphasis seems to have shifted from the 'threat' of developing countries to the 'threat' of Japan (a perception that has changed in a remarkably short period). Unfortunately, this probably does not mean that developing or NIC exporters have been let off the hook. All the signs are that protectionism has a capacity for spreading, however specifically it is intended to apply. Restraints on one product inevitably spread to others, for example, from televisions to television tubes. Restraints on one exporting country inevitably spread to others, for example from Japan to the NICs. And restraints by one importing country inevitably spread to others, for example USA restraints on Japanese cars have spread to Germany, Benelux and Canada. In respect of this last point, the evolution of the protectionist stance of the USA appears crucial to the EEC. The new USA Administration is strongly pro free-trade in rhetoric, though the practice so far is at best ambivalent, as in its reluctant and painful acquiescence in VERs on Japanese cars on the one hand, and its decision to end quotas on shoe imports on the other.

Notes

1 See, for instance, L. M. Gard and J. Riedel, 'Safeguard protection of industry in developed countries. Assessment of the implications for developing countries', *Weltwirtschaftliches Archiv*, September 1980.

2 See Helen Hughes and Jean Waelbroeck, 'Can developing-country exports keep growing in the 1980s?', *The World Economy*, June 1981, vol. 4, no. 2.

3 Drs. K. Koekkoek, Drs. J. Knol, Prof. L. Mennes, 'Protectionisme in Nederland', *ESB*, July 1981.

5

Who is More Preferred? An Analysis of the New Generalised System of Preferences

Ann Weston

At the beginning of 1981, in a climate of worldwide recession, the EEC renewed its Generalised System of Preferences (GSP) for a second decade, though with significant modifications. This took place with little public comment, yet when generalised tariff preferences for imports from developing countries were first introduced by the EEC in July 1971 (later followed by Japan, Norway, Sweden, Finland, New Zealand, Switzerland, Austria, Australia, Canada and finally USA) it was heralded as a major step forward in North-South relations. In principle the GSP offered ldc exporters the advantage of lower tariffs over dc exporters competing with them on most favoured nation (mfn) terms, and so was intended to stimulate ldc trade. Such preferential treatment had previously existed under special agreements (such as the Commonwealth Agreement or the Yaoundé Convention) but only for a limited number of countries and moreover the tariff preferences had to be reciprocated by the ldcs which were party to these agreements. Not only was the GSP to be offered to all ldcs without discrimination but also they did not have to offer dcs reciprocal treatment.

This lack of comment on the new GSP is unfortunate, because it is potentially important for ldc trade. There are several factors which may have diverted attention from the EEC's new scheme. First, as mfn tariffs are being cut following the conclusion of the Tokyo Round of Multilateral Trade Negotiations, it might be thought that the preferential margin which the GSP can offer ldcs is no longer significant and new initiatives are required to stimulate ldc exports. In fact the Tokyo Round tariff cuts were less extensive than expected – the weighted average tariff in the main OECD countries on ldc industrial products[1] fell by 25 % only, from 9.9 % to 7.9 % *ad valorem*. In the EEC market several products of importance to ldcs, not completely covered by the GSP, still face substantial mfn tariffs – for example gym shoes (20 %), cutlery (17 %), calculators (12 %), leather gloves (10 %), and leather footwear (8 %). For agricultural products the weighted average mfn tariff in the main OECD markets merely decreased from 11.7 % to 11.2 % – for one third of dutiable agricultural imports there were no tariff cuts at all. A few examples of agricultural products still facing high mfn duties in the EEC are honey (27 %), corned beef (26 %),[2] canned tunny (24 %), and rice (22 % plus a levy).[2] A second reason why the GSP may tend to be overlooked is that a large number of countries trade on better than GSP terms in the EEC market. The GSP beneficiaries come very near the bottom in the EEC's pyramid of privileges (see *Survey 1*, Chapter 4); exporters in nearly 70 ldcs (including those in the ACP group of the Lomé Convention, the Maghreb and the Mashreq who have special agreements with the EEC) as well as in many dcs (members of EFTA) enjoy lower tariffs. Thus the GSP only gives some 50 ldcs preference over the handful of dcs who actually trade on mfn terms with the EEC. But this small total overlooks the fact that the amount of EEC imports from these ldcs is still very large – and their terms of access an important issue. Third, the importance of tariffs is arguably being overshadowed by the increased use of non-tariff barriers against ldc imports, such as the quantity restrictions under the Multifibre Arrangement (MFA). If these barriers effectively restrict ldc imports, then in theory preferential tariff concessions merely result in a transfer of the customs revenue foregone by the EEC to ldc exporters; they cannot stimulate trade. A fourth, and more likely reason for the lack of comment on the new scheme is that it is complicated and riddled with uncertainties. In this respect, and despite the Commission's attempts to reform it, the new scheme closely resembles the old.

An assessment of the new scheme is important not only because it reveals a toughening attitude in the EEC to imports from ldcs, both the newly industrialising countries (NICs) and some of the poorer ldcs, but also because the EEC is the first to renew its GSP, and other donors may shape the modifications in their schemes on those of the EEC. The first section of this chapter begins with an examination of the old scheme and various proposals for its reform put forward by the ODI[3] and other bodies which undertook their own studies of the EEC's GSP – notably the UK House of Lords[4] – and also by various industrial groups in the EEC. This is followed by an outline of the new scheme as originally proposed by the Commission and then as finally adopted by the Council of Ministers. The final section evaluates the new scheme, in terms of its impact both on EEC trade (*ex ante*) and more generally on international trade issues, and considers whether further changes are needed.

The first GSP (1971–81)

Manufactured products (excluding textiles)

The first GSP applied to all manufactured and some agricultural imports from ldcs. All manufactured goods benefited from duty-free access to the EEC market, but for some 150 manufactured products this benefit was limited by tariff quotas (Ts) or ceilings which restricted the volume of goods receiving the preference. This limitation was designed to protect competitive industries in the EEC and the states whose interests the EEC was meant to protect under the Yaoundé Convention and later the Lomé Convention. These 150 products were divided into *sensitive*, *hybrid* and *semi-sensitive* products according to the degree of protection. In addition, restrictions (otherwise known as *butoirs* or maximum country amounts) were placed on the duty-free access which imports from any single ldc could enjoy. In most cases these were equal to a maximum 50% of the tariff quota or ceiling but the more competitive ldcs were given lower *butoirs* (often as low as 15%) in the case of hybrid products. Tariff quotas on sensitive products were also divided into shares for each EEC member state. With the exception of imports from the nine least developed countries outside the ACP group who were exempted from *butoirs* in 1977 and from quotas or ceilings in 1979, when any of these limits was reached, the full mfn duty was automatically reimposed, though in the case of semi-sensitive products a member state had to make a specific request before tariffs would be levied.

This complicated system inevitably made exporters (and importers) of sensitive, hybrid and some semi-sensitive products uncertain as to whether their goods would enter duty-free, unless they arrived in the EEC at the beginning of the year. It encouraged exporters, particularly in the more advanced ldcs, to race their goods to the EEC at the end of each year ready for the opening of the tariff quota on 1 January, with the result that many quotas were exhausted within a few days and for the rest of the year all imports paid the full mfn duty. In such cases the GSP could not stimulate trade. It was more like a lottery, offering a few lucky importers the chance of a windfall gain.

For non-sensitive products, GSP treatment was a lot more generous. Although they were also subject to ceilings and *butoirs* the formula[5] used to calculate these meant that they were rarely exceeded. Furthermore, they were not subject to regular surveillance, although the possibility remained that a member state might ask the Commission to reintroduce the mfn duty on imports from a particular ldc which exceeded the *butoir*, as happened on eleven occasions from 1975 to 1979.

As the date for GSP renewal approached, the various interested parties in the EEC put forward proposals for change. The arguments of those working to improve the value of the GSP for developing countries were typified by the proposals of ODI that the major priority for reform should be the sensitive products list and that the system of restriction should be simplified. In sharp contrast, several representatives of industries in the EEC (including chemicals, soluble coffee, vegetable oils) as well as L'Union des Industries de la Communauté Europèene felt there was a need for much greater differentiation between ldcs. They argued that some ldcs should 'graduate' from the group of beneficiaries, or if they were to continue to receive GSP they should begin to offer reciprocal concessions to EEC imports to their countries. In addition they suggested that the GSP should be withdrawn from any country operating 'unfair trading practices'. ODI argued against 'graduation' on the grounds that, while it had some validity as a concept, there would be major practical and political problems in implementing it.

Textile products

Until 1980, textile products were treated broadly as other industrial products with 30 in the sensitive category, 16 semi-sensitive and 50 non-sensitive. The major differences were, first, that for non-sensitive products the formula for calculating ceilings was less generous than for other industrial products, and second, that there was a more concerted effort to restrict GSP for the major suppliers (by means of separate tariff quotas or tighter *butoirs*). In 1980 the GSP was changed significantly for those textile products falling under the MFA and for the 21 ldcs with whom the EEC has bilateral agreements under the MFA. The major innovation was that each ldc was given its own fixed share of the TQ, based on its GNP per capita, past exports of that product to the EEC, and its quota under the MFA. For the very sensitive products the exporting country shares were subdivided between the member states. Products falling outside the MFA continued to be treated as in the past. Imports from the least developed countries (provided they met the rules of origin) were duty free throughout the year.

As long as textile trade with ldcs was to be regulated by quantity restrictions, tariffs could not restrict imports any more than preferential tariffs could promote them. But they could affect the level of prices paid by EEC consumers (or those received by the ldc exporters). It was therefore suggested by ODI that all ldc textile imports should be admitted duty-free up to the level of their individual quotas under the MFA.

Agricultural products

The GSP for agricultural products was quite different. The emphasis of the GSP in the EEC and elsewhere has predominantly been on promoting industrial exports from ldcs, to encourage their industrialisation. In its early days little attention was given to agricultural products, even if they were processed agricultural goods – only a handful were included in the

EEC scheme, and for most of these the GSP beneficiaries still had to pay some tariff. It soon became apparent that for many of the poorer ldcs agricultural goods might have a more important role to play in their development than industrial goods. With each annual review of the GSP therefore, the number of agricultural products covered was gradually increased until by 1980 it totalled over 320 items. According to the Commission the value of the goods covered rose from Eua 450 mn in 1974 to some Eua 1300 mn in 1980. The depth of tariff cut was also improved (from 3.6% in 1972 to 7.3% in 1977). For some products however, the preferential tariff margin in 1980 was still very low and the GSP tariff remained high – for example honey (25%), canned tunny (19%) and cloves (12%).

There was no predetermined limit on the amount of goods which could get GSP treatment (instead a safeguard clause allowed this to be withdrawn as necessary) except in six cases[6] which were subject to tariff quotas or ceilings. Unlike industrial products however, none of these tariff quotas included *butoirs*. In 1979 as a special concession to the nine least developed countries, the EEC made all of their agricultural exports which fell into the 320 categories covered by the GSP, completely duty-free, with the exception of Virginia tobacco and canned pineapple. In addition two new products (raisins and coffee beans) were included in the GSP but only for lldcs.

Further extension under the new GSP was recommended by several groups. The UK House of Lords Select Committee[7] and the British Importers' Confederation both suggested that extension should apply to products of interest to the poorer ldcs, ie a much larger group than the least developed ldcs; that the GSP tariffs should be further reduced, if not removed altogether; and that the tariff ceiling and quotas should be abolished.

Hence, there were three inter-related themes common to the various proposals for reform – simplification, graduation and protection. The need for simplification stemmed from the fact that the regulations governing the scope and use of the GSP had become so complex that they were considered to be a form of non-tariff barrier, which only the larger exporters and importers could afford to tackle. Graduation was largely an issue of equity: despite the system of *butoirs* the major beneficiaries of the scheme – the ten countries who accounted for 90% of imports under the GSP[8] – were still crowding out other ldcs. This was primarily a problem for the sensitive and hybrid products on which GSP access was restricted. It raised the more general question – whether there should be increased differentiation between ldcs. Some steps had already been taken in this direction with the special treatment of the lldcs. But should they be extended, and if so, how? Finally, there was the need, under certain circumstances, to protect ailing EEC industries from a surge in imports from GSP beneficiaries. This was perhaps the most controversial issue which, it was generally accepted, could not be ignored by policy-makers or by those making the proposals. The problem was deciding when protection against GSP imports was justified and what form it should take.

The new scheme

The different positions of various pressure groups, led the Commission to recommend a mixed package of reforms, which attempted to liberalise and simplify the GSP for the majority of ldcs, while making it more restrictive and complicated for imports of sensitive products from a number of vaguely defined 'more competitive ldcs'. They also wanted to include for the first time a number of semi-manufactured goods (yarns and leather items) and one agricultural product (basmati rice) of importance to poorer ldcs, as well as introducing larger tariff cuts for another group of agricultural products. No changes were proposed for textiles (other than to increase tariff quotas by 2% to allow for Greek entry to the EEC) on the grounds that the new system introduced in 1980 should be given time to operate before it could be evaluated and modified. They suggested extending the GSP for another 20 years though the structure proposed would only be for five years, subject to minor annual changes as necessary. In the past such annual changes had been subject to the approval of the Council of Ministers; this caused delays and often the regulations governing the new scheme were published only days before it was due to start. The Commission proposed that the details be delegated to a specially created management committee, such as existed for supervising imports under the MFA, with the Council of Ministers only taking decisions on the structure of the scheme and on matters of political importance.

With the important exception of the management committee, which was rejected outright, and the GSP's duration, which was halved to ten years, the thrust of the Commission's proposals was accepted by the Council of Ministers, though with some modification to the details. There are three major changes in the new scheme as it was finally agreed: new treatment for industrial products, reduction of GSP tariffs for some agricultural products, and inclusion of some new products. Of these the most important is the new treatment of industrial products. According to the Commission the new GSP for industrial products will be simpler, with two new categories – sensitive and non-sensitive – replacing the previous four. This view, however, ignores the special treatment of textiles, and the fact that differentiation has been introduced in the sensitive group (see below). Taking these into account, there are still four different categories of industrial products: *textiles*, two categories of sensitive products (which we shall call *very sensitive* and *less sensitive*), and *non-sensitive* items, which are described in detail in the Box opposite.

The new GSP classification for industrial products

Sensitive products

The new sensitive list of 128 products is roughly as large as the former sensitive, hybrid and semi-sensitive categories which together contained 124 items (in 1980), although one-third of the products are different. The list is also slightly different from that proposed by the Commission: 31 products were reclassified by the Council of Ministers into the non-sensitive group, but these were replaced by another 35 products. Fourteen products were added in response to a panic campaign by the UK chemicals industry and another 5 for the watch industry. In fact the chemicals industry had asked for a much longer list of products to be included but this was cut first by the UK government to 23 items and then by the Council.

For the 64 *very sensitive* products, certain competitive ldcs have been given individual, identical tariff quotas. As under the old GSP these are subdivided into member state shares. Once imports from a competitive ldc exceed its share, they have to pay the mfn duty. Imports from all other ldcs are treated as less sensitive.

There are 64 *less sensitive* products for which all ldcs have been given individual, identical tariff ceilings. Tariff ceilings differ from tariff quotas in two ways. First they are not divided into member state shares, and second, according to the Commission, they constitute minimal rather than maximal thresholds; when imports from a ldc reach its ceiling the mfn duty will not automatically be reimposed. Instead imports will continue to be given preferential treatment until a member state asks for it to be stopped. Imports from all other ldcs will tend to be duty-free all year, as if they were non-sensitive. It was expected that only a few ldcs would be affected, but in fact by June 1981 the mfn duty had been reimposed in more than 30 cases, many of them at the request of West Germany.

Non-sensitive products

Imports of the 1700 or so non-sensitive products from all ldcs face unrestricted duty-free treatment, though this can still be withdrawn at any time at the request of a member state after ten days' notice. The Commission had wanted to be able to guarantee ldcs GSP for their non-sensitive goods for a year at a time, suggesting that were it found necessary to restrict GSP imports from an ldc because of serious injury to an EEC industry, then restrictions, such as a tariff ceiling, would only be imposed at the beginning of the following year. But this proposal was opposed by all member states except Denmark on the grounds that it would reduce the EEC's ability to protect its industries from sudden increases in duty-free imports.

For the 64 *very sensitive* products the EEC has identified some 15 ldcs (see Table 5.1) as competitive suppliers which are considered no longer to need GSP and also to have crowded out other, less developed ldcs. The Commission's original proposal laid down criteria to define a competitive ldc based on the historical level of its exports but with an exemption for countries with a low GNP or heavily dependent on the export commodity in question. In the event, however, a more pragmatic approach has been adopted. Rather than exclude competitive ldcs completely they have each been given a separate, identical (except in two cases) duty-free tariff quota. As under the old GSP the tariff quotas are further subdivided between the ten EEC member states, and when imports of a very sensitive product from a competitive supplier exceed a member state's share, the full mfn tariff will be reimposed.

For less competitive ldcs, imports of very sensitive products are subject to separate tariff ceilings. The same applies to all imports of the 64 *less sensitive products* for which 'competitive ldcs' receive the same treatment as others. According to the UK Department of Trade, however, in each case only one or two ldcs are likely to reach the ceiling: these ldcs, and the number of tariff ceilings they are expected to exceed, are shown in Table 5.1. Finally, for non-sensitive products, there is in principle no differentiation between ldcs and no predetermined ceilings. In practice, though, imports of 44 non-sensitive products from twelve countries and a further six products from all ldcs are subject to special monthly (instead of the normal quarterly) surveillance and ceilings have been calculated for possible use against them.

To sum up, the GSP for industrial products remains highly complex with many different tiers of restriction, varying in degree and automaticity according to the perceived sensitivity of the product and the competitiveness of the ldc. For EEC importers, the main operators of the scheme, the situation is particularly complicated by the number of tariff quotas and ceilings, which have multiplied with the innovation of separate quotas and ceilings for each ldc. The EEC argues that this new system is more transparent for the ldcs: 'now that global ceilings are done away with, each beneficiary country can see in advance what advantages it is guaranteed and make the fullest use of them'.[9] While this may be true for those ldcs for whom duty-free treatment is virtually guaranteed throughout the year, in the 21 competitive ldcs individual exporters of sensitive products will still be forced to race their goods to the EEC in order to be sure of getting a share of their national quota (or ceiling), unless they are allotted shares in advance.

By contrast there have been few changes in the treatment of *agricultural products*, reflecting the general difficulty of introducing any changes in agricultural policy in the EEC. The Commission modestly proposed including only one new product – basmati rice – while increasing the tariff reduction on another nineteen products. Opposition from Italian rice growers and a UK-based rice processing company axed the proposal

Table 5.1 *Countries with restricted GSP treatment*

Country	Income per capita ($, 1979)[a]	Share of all GSP receiving imports (%, 1977)[b]	Number of products: Hitting *butoirs* & paying tariff (1980)[c]	Subject to tariff quotas (1981)	Likely to hit tariff ceilings (1981)[d]	Subject to special surveillance (1981)	Total (1981)
South Korea	1500	8.9	46	30	11	5	46
Hong Kong	4000	9.9	39	24	18	1	43
Brazil	1690	8.9	8	14	12	7	33
China	230[e]	na	20	7	25	13	45
Romania	1900	7.2	13	6	13	16	35
Singapore	3820	3.6	4	3	11	11	25
Chile	1690	na	1	2	3	1	6
Libya	8210	na	–	2	1	–	3
Malaysia	1320	10.5	2	2	4	–	6
Argentina	2280	3.3	2	4	1	4	9
Venezuela	3130	3.7	2	4	–	–	4
Indonesia	380	3.5	1	1	1	–	2
Philippines	600	3.9	8	1	6	–	7
Uruguay	2090	na	1	1	3	–	4
India	190	9.4	21	1	9	3	13
Pakistan	270	3.3	4	1	3	1	5
Mexico	1590	2.6	5	–	7	4	11
Thailand	590	3.5	8	–	4	–	4
Colombia	1010	0.6	–	–	2	–	2
Kuwait	17270	na	–	–	2	–	2
Bolivia	550	na	1	–	1	–	1
		82.8					

[a] World Bank Atlas 1980, preliminary estimates.
[b] Excluding Yugoslavia which now has a special trade agreement with the EEC.
[c] A Pitrone, *The EEC GSP Scheme in the 80s*, Agence Europeenne d'Informations, 1981, Vol. I, Annex 2, p. 12.
[d] Compiled from the Department of Trade's *Report on the Revision of the European Community's Scheme for 1981 and onwards*, 12 December 1980.
[e] 1978 figure.
na = not available.

on basmati rice, but instead three other products were added, the number of tariff cuts was extended to 42, and the quotas continue to be global (ie not divided between ldcs) as in the old GSP. Suggestions by Denmark, the Netherlands, and the UK that the least developed countries be exempted from the tariff quotas on tobacco and canned pineapple were rejected.

Evaluation of the new GSP

These changes in the GSP can be evaluated in two ways. First, how far does the new system represent a liberalisation of trade? This involves comparing the new tariff quotas and minimal thresholds with duty-free imports allowed under the old scheme. Second, there are the broader issues raised by the new GSP, in particular the increased differentiation between ldcs, and implications of this for future trade negotiations. This section deals with each question in turn and concludes by putting forward a list of changes which might be incorporated in the GSP in the course of its next annual review.

It is difficult to calculate *ex ante* to what extent the new GSP is more generous than in the past. This is partly because it is not clear whether the calculation should be based on the position of an individual ldc, of a competitive ldc, or of ldcs as a whole. The introduction of separate quotas and ceilings encourages one to think in terms of individual ldcs but, as explained in the Box below, there are a number of imponderables which completely bedevil calculation. Another way of evaluating the new GSP for industrial products is to compare the new tariff quotas and ceilings with the old *butoirs*. For most of the tariff quotas (roughly three-quarters) there have been increases of 2 %, apparently to take account of Greece joining the EEC. In real terms, however, this represents a cut in GSP coverage for the countries concerned. For the remaining very sensitive products[10] the tariff quotas have been placed at levels well below the old *butoirs* – often by as much as 30 % in current terms, nearer 40 % in real terms. Special quotas, 12 % above the old *butoirs*, have been calculated for two of the poorer ldcs which have been singled out as competitive suppliers of footwear, India and Pakistan. The picture is broadly similar for the tariff ceilings as for tariff quotas, though there have been a number of larger increases (of up to 12 %).

The question which remains unanswered is what effect this new system will have on the less competitive and therefore unrestricted ldcs. The EEC believes that the increased restrictions on GSP for competitive ldcs has shifted the balance in favour of less well organised exporters.[11] But many critics argue that these exporters will not be able to take advantage of the increased opportunities open to them – they need improvements in their productive capacity before they can take advantage of improved tariff access – and that the EEC's package will simply result in a fall in the total amount of duty-free imports. Clearly it will take at least one or two years

Problems in evaluation of the new GSP

In the past the value of the GSP 'offer' was calculated as the sum of the global tariff quotas and ceilings on sensitive, hybrid, semi- and non-sensitive products. Every year this offer was increased, largely as a result of the automatic increase in ceilings on non-sensitive products (with the periodic updating of the reference year used to calculate these ceilings). For the three sensitive categories increases were more discretionary, depending on the state of the EEC industry in question and the world economy.

The Commission does not attempt to quantify *ex ante* the duty-free opportunities available under the new GSP. This can only be roughly and laboriously calculated by multiplying the number of ldcs exporting each product by the level of the respective tariff ceiling (or quota). For example, to take the case of *protective gloves* (falling in tariff heading 4203BI), one supplier (Hong Kong) faces a tariff quota of 2.8 mn Eua while other suppliers each face a tariff ceiling of Eua 2.8 mn. As there are nine other ldc suppliers (according to 1979 import figures) and as the ceilings are a minimum, this means that had the 1981 scheme been operating in 1979, at least Eua 28 mn worth of gloves could have been imported duty-free; more than the Eua 23 mn actually receiving duty-free treatment in 1979.

Alternatively, using the latest figures for total imports from GSP beneficiaries, for each product we can deduct those imports on which duty would have been paid. The problem is knowing whether or not ldcs exceeding their ceiling will continue to receive GSP. If they do, then (to continue with our example) some Eua 31 mn worth of gloves would have received GSP; if, however, the mfn duty is reimposed immediately, then the amount of duty-free gloves would have fallen to Eua 23 mn. These examples should illustrate why it is difficult to estimate the value of the new GSP to ldcs as a whole.

before the impact of the new GSP on the EEC's industrial imports will be apparent.

The changes in the new GSP for agricultural products are of little substance. Four new products have been included, but for three of these (whole thyme, crushed thyme and bay leaves) it is not possible to trace any imports from GSP beneficiaries in EEC import statistics for 1979. Most imports come from more preferred suppliers (Spain, Morocco and Turkey), so that the small tariff reductions are unlikely to stimulate imports from GSP sources. A potentially more important product, fishmeal, has only been included for the least developed countries, of whom none are yet exporters to the EEC. If they do begin to export it to the EEC, lldcs will be required to pay a duty on fishmeal of 9% (compared to the mfn rate of 13%) whereas all their other agricultural exports covered by the GSP are duty-free. In other words, with fishmeal, the EEC has introduced a new category of product into its GSP.

The 42 agricultural products for which the preferential margin has been increased are also fairly minor ldc exports: in 1979 ten items were not exported by ldcs to the EEC, and in less than ten did exports exceed Eua 1 mn. For the largest item, unroasted decaffeinated coffee, the tariff cut is very small – from 10% to 9% – probably to protect ACP as much as EEC interests. Similar one percentage cuts apply to most other cases, and in no instance is the cut more than three per cent, although six products have been made duty-free with the removal of the remaining very small 'nuisance' tariffs. The value of these additional preferential tariff cuts has been offset by parallel mfn tariff cuts on 44 agricultural items under the Multilateral Trade Negotiations. As a result the average preferential margin for agricultural products in the EEC's 1981 scheme is 7.4%, exactly the same as in 1980.[12]

In terms of broader issues, there are two important features in the EEC's new GSP, which are interlinked, namely increasing differentiation between ldcs and increasing bilateralisation of EEC-ldc trade relations. Differentiation between ldcs goes against the original and basic principle of the GSP, that it should be generalised to all ldcs without distinction. With time it has become clear that differentiation is as necessary in trade policy towards ldcs as in aid policy – and most GSP schemes have incorporated more preferential treatment for lldcs. The contentious issue is whether to help the less competitive ldcs it is necessary to curtail GSP for the more competitive ldcs, or whether some other form of assistance to the former would be more suitable. Clearly the more competitive ldcs only crowd out others if the EEC decides to restrict its GSP package – an alternative to restricting competitive ldcs, therefore, would be to end all restrictions on GSP.

Increasing differentiation between ldcs has been strengthened by the EEC's desire to bilateralise its trade relations with ldcs, in an attempt to penalise those countries which restrict imports from the EEC. A statement by the Council of Ministers attached to the text of the new GSP suggests that each year the levels of individual tariff quotas and ceilings will be fixed according to how open each ldc is to imports from the EEC. Although the EEC (and other donors) has always insisted that the GSP is non-negotiable, not legally binding, and non-reciprocal, this no longer appears true. Under the new scheme the EEC has been able to single out Brazil and penalise it for its restrictions on EEC imports by increasing the number of Brazilian products likely to pay mfn tariffs to 33, compared to the 8 hitting *butoirs* in 1980.

Conclusions

Now into its second decade the GSP remains an active tool of EEC trade policy towards ldcs falling outside the Lomé Convention. To some it may be surprising that at a time of continuing recession and growing unemployment no product or ldc has been withdrawn from the scheme. For many ldcs, however, the GSP remains of disappointing value to their export efforts; it is inadequate, insecure and complicated. Furthermore, it has come to be used as a political tool – to divide ldcs, by turning the less developed against the more developed, and to persuade the latter to liberalise their imports from the EEC. If the GSP is to meet its original objectives namely to promote development by expanding the demand for (largely manufactured) exports, further changes are required in the EEC's scheme. These could be introduced in the course of the annual reviews, or at the end of 1985 when a more extensive review is planned.

For industrial products changes are needed to make the GSP more transparent and secure. In particular the restriction of GSP by product and by country should only be allowed under certain clearly defined criteria where imports under GSP can be shown to be damaging EEC industries. A body similar to the USA Trade Commission or the Australian Industrial Assistance Commission should be set up to consider in public requests by EEC producers, importers, and even ldc exporters, for changes in the amount of imports given GSP treatment. Special consideration should be given to the poorer ldcs, maybe to the extent of excluding them from any restrictions, as are the lldcs. Where tariff quotas or ceilings are found to be necessary, these should be increased automatically every year at least in line with inflation. Member state shares, which are contrary to the principle of free circulation in the EEC, should be abolished by replacing tariff quotas with ceilings which would help to simplify the GSP. For agricultural products, there is still considerable scope for improvements both in the product coverage and the depth of tariff cut. Changes in recent years have been cosmetic – there are still many products of importance to the poorer ldcs which are either excluded or still pay high tariffs under the GSP, ranging from fresh fruit and cocoa products to canned fish. To sum up, if the EEC wants to demonstrate its continued support of ldc exports at a time of world recession, rather than focussing on the problems of redistributing the benefits of GSP between ldcs, it should consider ways of increasing the GSP package overall.

Notes

1 Excluding textiles which are quantity restricted and for which tariff cuts can therefore have little effect.

2 These are not included in the EEC's GSP.

3 A. Weston, V. Cable, A. Hewitt, *The EEC's Generalised System of Preferences – Evaluation and Recommendations for Change*, ODI, London, 1980.

4 House of Lords, Select Committee on the European Communities, *Generalised System of Tariff Preferences*, HMSO, London, 1980.

5 Ceilings were composed of a basic amount (the value of EEC imports of a product from all GSP beneficiaries in a base year) *plus* a supplementary amount (5% of EEC imports of that product from all other sources in the latest year for which statistics were available).
6 Cocoa butter, instant coffee, two types of tobacco and two types of canned pineapple.
7 House of Lords, Select Committee on the European Communities, 1980, op. cit.
8 In 1977 these were Yugoslavia, Malaysia, Hong Kong, India, Brazil, Korea, Romania, the Philippines, Venezuela and Singapore.
9 European Commission, *European File* no 9/81, p. 7.
10 Including tanned leather, leather travel goods, leather clothing, footwear, plywood, and radio receivers.
11 See for instance, EEC, *Official Journal* L354, 29 December 1980, on the new GSP: 'Whereas use of the preferential advantages in the years 1971 to 1979 was concentrated in a limited number of products and beneficiary countries . . . it is therefore necessary to ensure a better distribution of the preferential advantages in order to provide practical assistance for the industrial development of a greater number of developing countries, especially the least developed . . . (and) to take account of the limits to the Community market's absorption capacity and the existence of Community production . . .'
12 UNCTAD, *Sixth General Report on the Implementation of the Generalised System of Preferences*, TD/B/C. 5/73, 1981, p. 8.

6

The Political Economy of The Multifibre Arrangement

Chris Farrands

The European Economic Community (EEC) provides a common framework for the organisation and representation of European textile interests in international diplomacy. The powerful set of instruments it has evolved for this purpose can only be understood in the context of the domestic pressures and industrial structure of the Community. The perceptions and interests of member governments and Community institutions have evolved against a background of rapid industrial, market and technical change. A small group of newly industrialising countries (NICs) have offered a potent challenge which, together with strong competition from other developed countries, have led to increasing protection by the EEC. But that protection has been aimed as much at the Third World as a whole as at these specific NIC and developed country antagonists. The Community has become an industrial and diplomatic actor of great power, with the ability to act as the dictator of the scope and pattern of developing countries' textile and clothing industries. Yet the economic rationale for EEC policy is dubious, and the political process which produces it is corporatist, uncertainly controlled and, whatever other protestations may be made about a desire to help the South, has a malign influence on the developing world. It is in cases of trade policy that the gap between rhetoric and the real impact of the Community can perhaps best be measured.

The importance of the textile and clothing industry

The textile and clothing industries have a traditional importance in the EEC. They are the third largest employment sector in Britain and France, and the largest industrial employer in Ireland. Productivity per person employed has grown by about 50 % in both sectors since 1973. But the number of firms has declined steadily, by about 15 % in each sector in the same period. And employment has slumped: approaching two million

Table 6.1 *Selected structural developments in textiles and clothing*

		1973	*1974*	*1975*	*1976*	*1977*	*1978*	*1979*
Employees ('000)	textiles	1 848	1 754	1 629	1 573	1 525	1 457	1 415
	clothing	1 276	1 204	1 146	1 094	1 055	1 011	1 002
Firms[a]	textiles	14 842	14 483	13 780	13 360	13 012	12 833	12 594*
	clothing	15 708	15 304	14 428	14 078	13 445	13 467	13 384*
Value Added (Eua mn, constant prices, 1973)	textiles	10 986*	11 872	10 923	11 655	11 344	11 519*	12 468*
	clothing	5 562*	5 963	5 928	5 870	5 931	6 188*	6 611*
Value Added per Person (Eua, constant prices 1973)	textiles	5 946*	6 768	6 705	7 409	7 439	7 906*	8 811*
	clothing	4 361*	4 953	5 173	5 366	5 622	6 121*	6 598*
Value Added (Eua mn, current prices)	textiles	10 986*	12 711*	12 534	14 090	14 581	15 570*	17 400*
	clothing	5 562*	6 385	6 769	7 126	7 606	8 300*	9 190*
Value Added per Person (Eua, current prices)	textiles	5 946*	7 249*	7 675	8 955	9 721*	10 832*	12 470*
	clothing	4 361*	5 374*	6 008	6 560	7 264*	8 189*	9 077*
Investment (Eua mn, 1970 prices)[b]	textiles	1 271	1 181	905	919	835	850*	970*
	clothing	292	240	201	215	217	230*	240*

* Estimate
[a] Only enterprises of 20 or more employees included.
[b] Subject to slight revision.

Source: European Commission, *The European Community's Textile Trade*, 44/81, Brussels, EEC Commission, April 1981.

jobs were lost in the 1970s, with a decline of 25 % between 1973 and 1979 in total employment.[1] In 1980 a further 100,000 jobs were lost in Britain alone. The overall pattern of industrial change is shown in Table 6.1, and the pattern of job loss in Table 6.2, which show clearly that the industry has been subject to drastic changes. In 1980, employment fell by a further 45,000 in textiles and 43,000 in clothing. It has responded by major adjustments. But it is arguable that adjustments have been at the expense of developing producers at least as much as at the expense of workers in the EEC member states.

There have been three main causes of change. Firstly, technical changes have concentrated production on larger scale, more capital intensive production, especially in textiles, with high investment required. This has suited the richer industries of Germany and the United States and Japan, or the more flexible industries of Hong Kong and South Korea, rather than those of Britain, Belgium and France. Secondly, the recession has hit demand, and has made low cost items more attractive to consumers. And thirdly, imports have been a major challenge to some EEC producers. But many imports have come from other developed producers inside and outside the EEC, rather than from ldcs. Italy has seized a major part of

Table 6.2 *Employment and job loss in the major EEC textile and clothing industries* ('000)

	1972	*1973*	*1974*	*1975*	*1976*	*1977*	*% loss 1972–77*
Textiles							
W. Germany	448	425	387	351	338	328	−27
France	406	398	387	363	353	341	−16
Italy	377	374	364	345	335	317	−16
Netherlands	64	59	57	51	47	43	−33
Belgium	88	87	83	74	71	63	−28
UK	524	518	504	458	454	448	−14
Ireland	23	23	22	19	20	20	−13
Denmark	22	21	18	16	16	15	−32
EEC total	1 950	1 905	1 821	1 678	1 635	1 577	−19
Clothing							
W. Germany	362	350	302	280	263	256	−29
France	307	304	290	280	280	280	−9
Italy	216	220	211	206	196	na	−5
Netherlands	49	44	35	29	26	23	−53
Belgium	65	66	64	59	53	48	−26
UK	340	327	322	307	303	295	−13
EEC total	1 366	1 343	1 264	1 196	1 156	1 123	−18
EEC TOTAL	3 316	3 248	3 085	2 874	2 791	2 700	−19

Source: European Commission, *General guidelines for a textile and clothing industry policy*, COM (78) 362 final.

the EEC market for ladies tights which was dominated by France in the recent past. The USA has made major inroads into the EEC market, especially in the last two years when a federal subsidy on energy gave an effective subsidy to synthetic fibre producers whose raw material is oil. The USA has taken about half of the British carpet market. In addition, of course, there have been imports from ldcs including the major East Asian countries, but of the poorer Third World, only India has a major share in the EEC's market (see Table 6.3). Yet while rich states get the markets, poor economies feel that they get the blame.

Table 6.3 *Growth rates for major suppliers to EEC markets: all MFA products*

Country	*'000 tonnes (1979)*	*1975–79 Average annual change (%)*
Bilateral Agreements		
Hong Kong	134.9	2.2
South Korea	80.0	7.6
India	74.5	0.9
Taiwan	60.8	2.3
Brazil	58.0	6.6
China	40.7	3.8
Pakistan	35.1	3.6
Malaysia	13.8	1.0
Singapore	13.8	0.7
Sri Lanka	2.2	333.3[a]
Preferential Countries		
Greece	100.8	7.2
Portugal	81.0	15.9
Spain	58.0	7.7
Malta	11.4	11.4
Cyprus	2.2	333.3[a]
Industrialised		
USA	211.5	13.4
Australia	78.5	8.9
Switzerland	71.1	10.8

[a] Calculated from a reported very high increase from a low base – 1000 % over three years.

Source: European Commission.

The evolution of the MFA

The EEC has developed a textile policy against the background of the evolution of the Multifibre Arrangements (MFA). The MFA grew out of the 1962 Long Term Agreement for cotton products, which, largely under pressure from USA, set limits on sales to developed economies of Asian textile products in particular. In 1973 this was replaced by the MFA, which was welcomed by developing textile producers on the grounds that they had a more equitable role in its negotiation; that they had a new Textile Surveillance Body which could arbitrate on their complaints as they arose; and, most important of all, because the Arrangement allowed a 6 % per year growth in their exports into developed markets. For their part, developed countries, including the EEC, welcomed the 1973 MFA because it extended the limits of the cotton agreement to other textile products including the rapidly growing synthetics sector. It provided a structure of special quotas on 'sensitive' products where imports might do particular harm to their own industry, and yet seemed more consistent with GATT principles than the alternative anarchy of many different textile trade deals.

The 1973 MFA was thus a relatively liberal compromise which assumed that developing states could have a larger role in western economies which would themselves be growing quickly. Within a year this optimism was shattered. Between 1973 and 1977 EEC economies grew on average at half the rate of the late 1960s. Demand for textiles actually fell in 1974–5. In the event, therefore, the 1973 MFA was a disaster for the EEC's industry. Or, more accurately, the period in which it operated was. While other developed countries operated the MFA effectively from the start, the EEC was slow to implement it, uncertain in its approach, lacked the information to act effectively and, at least in the minds of European industrialists, lacked the will to be effective and the competence to see what was happening. Third World exports to the EEC grew disproportionately: Hong Kong's textile sales to the USA grew at about 4 % in 1973–7; to the Community they grew at about 42 %. In addition, there was extensive fraud, with industrially produced cotton goods, mainly from India, being labelled as 'folkloric' or handloom products in order to escape quotas.

However, while the EEC's textile industry has faced strong competition from ldc imports, the competition has been concentrated only on some countries, and in certain product areas (especially in cheaper clothing). Between 1968 and 1977, developing countries increased their market share of woven non-cotton textile products from 9.8 % to 17 % of the world market, while the EEC's market share fell.[2] The EEC's share of total world imports between 1973 and 1977 grew from 45 % to 50 %, while that of the USA fell by half from 4.5 % to around 2 %. Not only did Community imports of these products grow, but the EEC took a larger share of Third World exports than did other developed economies. By 1978 the Community as a whole had a clothing trade deficit of $3,274 mn with all countries, while the four major developing producers (South Korea, Hong Kong, Taiwan and India) had a clothing trade surplus of $9,936 mn. But these figures are deceptive in several ways: in 1978, USA sold more 'sensitive category' goods to the Community than did any other country; Hong Kong, the second largest exporter to the EEC, had a clothing surplus of $3,145 mn but a textile deficit of $841 mn, since it imports textiles, partly from the EEC, to manufacture and export. Thus, while the EEC does have a real problem adjusting to imports of clothing from ldcs, that problem needs to be seen in relation to an overall surplus in manufactured goods where textiles is an exception, to technical and other market changes in the industry, and to textile trade with developed countries like the USA and the Mediterranean.

Despite the fact that imports from developed countries and technical changes were separately more important sources of change in the Community than Third World low cost imports, it was the Third World producers who formed the main target when the MFA came up for renewal in 1977. This can be explained partly because the growth rates in their sales attracted the attention of industrial lobbies, although they started from low bases. But it was also partly because they made a much easier target than, for example, the United States, where tough textile industries had the strength and will to get retaliatory measures through Congress if they were hit. The negotiating structure of the MFA favoured the Community, which made its acceptance of the renewal of the MFA conditional on the satisfactory negotiation of bilateral deal with each of the developing producers. In such talks the EEC could effectively pick off developing country exporters one by one. Despite bitter complaints from Hong Kong, predictions of disaster in India and Singapore, and a relatively concerted *démarche* by the cotton producers in December 1977, Community negotiators got substantially what they wanted. Developing countries were willing to accept the quotas suggested rather than the threatened alternative of no quotas at all.

The 1977 MFA succeeded in cutting back imports of sensitive products from developing countries: in 1978–9 sensitive imports from South Korea fell by 3.7 %, while between 1976 and 1979 imports from India and Hong Kong fell by 0.9 % and 2.2 % respectively.[3] Combined with a small increase in level of demand in the Community in 1979, this encouraged optimism in the EEC industry that if import restrictions could be maintained, and government help for job saving and new investment increased, the short-term prospects were good. In the event, however, this optimism was not justified. While the 1977 MFA hit its designated targets, the major developing producers, a series of other challenges found much of European industry wanting.

Between 1977 and 1981, the European economy failed to grow as fast as the optimistic forecasts of 1978–9 had suggested. As a result, 'temporary' measures have appeared increasingly permanent, and European industry has called for a yet tougher MFA to last not five years, but ten. The oil price increases of 1979–80 have not made life easier for those parts of the textile industry which use oil products as raw materials. Imports from the USA have grown into an increasingly serious problem. The difficulties of managing textile relations with the Mediterranean countries are increasing and will inevitably grow more rather than less. Only the 'Third World challenge', and some problems with low cost East European exporters have been dealt with effectively.

The textile lobbies

EEC relations on textile and clothing trade policy cannot be explained without looking at the internal politics and the perceptions of member states, industrial groups and European institutions. Throughout almost all of the period between 1973 and 1981 there has been close cooperation between unions and industrial groups in matters of textile trade policy. One would expect their interests to coincide on these issues even where they are engaged in arguments on issues of pay, conditions or redundancy terms. This unity has given strength to pressure group campaigns. It has been fostered by coordinating groups at national and sectoral level which exercise great influence even though they are generally small in size. They owe their influence to their access to governments and civil servants. This access is in part the result of their special technical expertise. Bodies like the German *Gesamtextil* and the Knitting Industries Federation in Britain have information about techniques, market prospects, patterns of trade and demand which only those in the industry can supply. If governments are to get this information and understand it, they need regular contacts with industrial representatives which are effective bases for the education of governments in the interests of industry. Where unemployment is a major issue there are additional pressures for co-operation and consultation. Fear that backbenchers or allies in a coalition might ask why industry has not been consulted are often simple but effective grounds for meetings between governments and industrialists. All EEC countries have the equivalents of the British sector working parties which look at the technical and structural problems of industry. The intimacy of trades unions and governments vary, but they can be very close, as, for example, when junior trade and industry ministers attended as a matter of course meetings of the TUC's Textile, Clothing and Footwear Committee for much of the 1974–79 UK Labour government's term.

The most intimate relations between government and industry develop where government finance is committed. With one exception, all the major EEC governments give subsidies to their textile and clothing industries. Some of these are massive. They vary, however, in form. It is difficult to gauge the scale of this intervention and to compare different national schemes. One estimate is that in Italy and the Netherlands subsidies totalled $302 and $300 a head respectively in the clothing industries in the mid-1970s, while in Britain the figure was $200, and in France and Belgium it was about $50. The exception is Germany, which gave subsidies of only about $2 a head, mostly through regional assistance.[4]

There are good reasons for believing that these figures for France and Italy are underestimates. Moreover, they do not include such under-the-table help as subsidised export credit.

Italy has the most widespread government support, with massive investment and close co-operation between economic planners in government and industry. The French planning office and the British Industry Department are similarly involved, though the sums are rather smaller. In Ireland, government and industry became used to collaboration in the 1960s, when it was recognised that entry to the EEC would mean lifting the tight protection which had shielded the country's industry since the 1930s. So a plan of investment and capacity reduction was jointly arranged. This support has continued into the 1970s. While Ireland's textile industry is important in Dublin, it is relatively small within the EEC, and in consequence government support measures which in larger EEC economies would attract the attention of the EEC's Competition Directorate operate freely. Similarly, other major producers give substantial help to their industries in one form or another, so that it is clear there is no such thing as a free market for clothing and textiles. The German association, *Gesamtextil*, has produced a detailed study of the ten major producers, arguing that unfair competition is subsidised by abnormal government practices in a way which hits the poorest most, since they generally cannot compete with this competition.[5]

Gesamtextil has, perhaps understandably, in view of the fact that its national government is the exception, found itself playing the role of the jealous poor sister amongst European industry groups. It has several times complained to the European Commission about the support given to other countries' industries, most importantly in 1979 and 1980 against Italian and Belgian government aids respectively. This pattern of suspicion amongst industry groups is not limited to Germany however; after all, firms and groups which agree about the dangers of foreign competition are themselves in competition. In autumn 1980, the French government introduced a system of import licences against Italian textile products. This short-lived restraint on trade resulted from concern in French industry about the volume of Italian exports to France. It achieved little in itself, but illustrates clearly the tensions that recession and unemployment have brought to the 'Common Market'. It is often easier to blame developing countries' competition than it is to live with competition within the Community.

These reasons for intimacy between national governments and industry, are reinforced in many cases by style, inclination, and political motives. The British Labour government's view of the industry was coloured by its political vulnerability in the House of Commons, and by its programme of co-operation with the trades union movement through the Social Contract. The UK industry and trade departments have fostered their own style of corporatism since they were reorganised by Edward Heath. In France, trade policy has been particularly receptive to the textile lobby's cause. In both countries, the treasury, which might perhaps have been more interested in free trade at other times, has apparently accepted protection on broad balance of payments grounds. French Gaullist deputies have brought pressure to bear in the Assemblée Nationale on a government looking for their support on other issues. Coalition governments in Italy and Belgium have proved amenable to pressure from textile constituencies. Coalition politics appear to work in the opposite way in Germany: it is the minority party in the German government which presses for liberal trade (representing few industrial interests), and while the Social Democrats are less intervention-minded than their British or French counterparts, they would have been more active if unrestrained by the Free Democrats' liberalism.

It is fair to say that those governments which have been most responsive to industrial lobbying have been those most predisposed to interventionist and protective public policy, regardless of political labels. One interesting exception to this rule, however, appears to have been Mrs Thatcher's government in UK. The Conservatives were elected on an anti-interventionist ticket in an election campaign where they made strident attacks on the corporatism of their predecessors. Conservative leaders, above all Sir Keith Joseph, appeared to think that the growth of the corporate economy was as reversible as it was undesirable. In its first year, a series of comments from ministers including Sir Keith and the Trade Secretary, John Nott, suggested to industry that it had had long enough to adjust to world competition, and that, in their view, industry was using the MFA regime to avoid necessary change. Instructions were apparently given to civil servants to restrain their corporatist impulses. However, since June 1980 there have been no more such statements, and the British government advocated a tough line in the MFA negotiations of 1981. Conservative MPs from marginal seats in Lancashire and West Yorkshire must take some credit for this change, but so too must the persevering continuity of civil service views. The trade associations, especially the British Textile Confederation, made a 'really major effort' to 'educate' the government. And no doubt the realities of unemployment and the relative difficulties in viable alternatives have had an important effect in sponsoring this quiet but considerable U-turn.

At the European level, a complicated pattern of interest group politics is represented through three channels:[6] there are sector groups such as CIRFS, the synthetics group, and *Mailleurop*, the knitting industry institution; there are national groups such as those mentioned above; and there are union groups, including the European Trades Union Congress (ETUC) and the International Federation of Hosiery and Knitwear Unions. All three kinds of groups (there are to my certainly incomplete knowledge at least 16 European-wide industry co-ordinating groups) have access to the EEC Commission. Interest groups recognise the importance of the national governments and the Council of Ministers in EEC policy-making, and their first resort is still to national government.

Nonetheless, there is in addition an important and distinct European level of pressure group politics. At its apex is COMITEXTIL, the European industry's overall co-ordinating committee. This body, which was set up in 1969, represents all the major national and sector groups. The Commission, having represented European countries in textile discussions as part of the Kennedy Round of the GATT, and having been bombarded by contrary advice and information, helped to encourage the establishment of a group which could represent the European textile and clothing industries with one voice. COMITEXTIL, though small and constitutionally powerless, is expert and wields great influence. It provided technical advice throughout the 1977 MFA talks on an 'almost daily' basis, and for part of the talks with Asian producers sent its two chief officers as technical advisers with the Commission's negotiating team.

It is not possible to isolate the different levels of government policy-making from each other. In any case, chambers of commerce, regional union activities, informal consultation over lunch and in corridors all have additional effects. European policy towards developing countries on textile and clothing trade policy emerges from a process in which there are powerful pressures for trade control at every level. That process is all the more important because in general it is now thoroughly rehearsed, and because patterns of policy and thinking are harder to change to the extent that, over a decade, they have become habitual.

There are interest groups which have sought to challenge this apparently established consensus. They have done so on a variety of grounds, including free trade, Third World development, the protection of importers and retailers, and the protection of European exports from retaliation. So far they have had rather limited success. The German government is more predisposed to sympathise with free trade interest groups, and the liberal Economics Minister, Count Lambsdorff, has won their praise especially by a controversial speech in May 1978 attacking protectionism in general. Yet anti-protectionist groups which might lend weight to criticisms of the established MFA are generally politically weak. They are deeply divided on issues of principle and the interests which provoke their attitude to the MFA. Co-operation amongst them has been weak, especially by comparison with that achieved by those wanting protection.

Three governments have taken a more liberal line on textiles than the other EEC states: West Germany, the Netherlands and Denmark. Their public and political elites are more sympathetic towards Third World development concerns, and they do not have the same regional problems that other EEC members suffer (although even in rich Denmark, the small textile and clothing industry is located in the relatively poor North Jutland area). Because their economies have been in general relatively strong, and because textiles are relatively less significant in their overall contribution to national production, they coped more easily with the high proportionate rate of job loss which they have suffered. But, as noted in Chapter 4, the most important reason for their position in the textile talks has been their structural relations with European and world trade: Holland and Denmark in particular are small, open economies which depend to such an extent on external trade that they see few gains for themselves in restrictions. Germany, with a larger economy and a textile industry which employs half a million workers, also sees itself as dependent on trade in industrial goods so that sectoral restrictions are regarded as more damaging than advantageous. The German industry has also become increasingly dependent on outward processing, whereby partially completed goods are sent abroad for finishing in countries where labour is cheaper. This practice, which is considered in detail in Chapter 7, has become the subject of union criticism, makes trade figures harder to interpret, and also militates against trade protection.

Cutting across the national and European political processes are the major multinationals. In the 1960s, as the market for synthetic products grew rapidly, large chemical companies not only came to dominate synthetic textiles but bought their way into clothing, the wool industry, and distribution. During the recession of the 1970s, they often had cause deeply to regret these purchases as they became the source of large losses. Courtaulds, Montedison and Rhone-Poulenc have had bitter experience in this respect. On the whole, the structure of the European industry has become more concentrated across the board, but this concentration has been more accentuated in the capital intensive, larger scale operations of textiles, while the smaller scale, fragmented, clothing industry remains vulnerable to bankruptcy, difficult to organise and harder to co-ordinate against technical change. Eleven multinational companies dominate the European synthetics and textiles market. They have direct access to the Commission and the ear of the governments. Co-ordination has not been easy as they are competitors, with different interests and patterns of investment outside the EEC, but nevertheless they have co-operated in important respects.

Regional problems are one of the chief causes of the political sensitivity of textile and clothing problems. The industries tend through much of Europe to be concentrated in weak, run-down areas. In Northern Ireland, the most pointed example, the major alternative industry, shipbuilding, has also been in a long decline. In Lorraine and Wallonia, the decline in textiles is matched by that in coal and steel. In the Mezzogiorne and in many south Lancashire cotton towns, there is no alternative industry. Where alternative new industries have been brought in, usually with government help, they have not always prospered, as the collapse of the television industry in Skelmersdale illustrates. The problems of managing the textile industry are far more serious because, by and large, it lies outside the central 'golden triangle' of the EEC. A comparison of the decline of the traditional Jewish tailoring business of London and Leeds illustrates this point: in the former there has been rapid change to other industries; in the latter, not the poorest of towns, there has been collapse and stagnation. Outside Lorraine and Wallonia, the political consequences of this regional collapse have been less severe than might have been expected (excluding Ulster, where the causes of the troubles are quite separate, though their solution is certainly not helped by unemployment). But politicians are nervous that this may not continue, and the urge to preserve regional political stability (or even law and order) presses on other motives for the special protection of textiles. Equally, it is arguable that one reason why Denmark, Holland and Germany have been less sympathetic towards the protection of textiles is that their regional problems lack the scale of those of the other member states.

EEC decision-making

European textile policy as a whole is compounded from these elements. Within the decision-making process, a number of forces moderate the general tendency, but since 1973 that tendency has been consistently for an increase in protection. The EEC Commission plays a central role in the evolution of policy. It is, in effect, the only institution which can take a European-wide view of textile policy. And the Commission negotiates on behalf of the Community in the MFA. Member states and industry have continued to regard the Commission with great suspicion. It is seen as weak, vacillating, technically incompetent and remote from the issues of textile and clothing industries. These criticisms were, in general, justified in the early period of the MFA. Commission staff involved in textile policy were rather ill-informed and slow to deal with the problems which arose. More recently, however, the standard of Commission handling of textile policy has been high, especially in international negotiations. But the Commission has also been affected by a deep political division which mirrors the division amongst member states. The Industry Commissioner, Viscount Davignon, has taken up the cause of industrial regeneration in areas such as steel and textiles. He has been supported in putting forward actively interventionist schemes by some colleagues, including the past President, Roy Jenkins, but his views have been opposed by others, including the Budget Commissioner, Mr Tugendhat, and the former Competition Commissioner, M. Vouel. These divisions are most easily put in this personalised way, but they reflect very important differences of view about the future of industry and trade policy within the Community. And, since the Community has only a limited industrial policy, trade policy has been used as a substitute for a more fully developed and more successful internal industrial policy.[7]

These divisions within the EEC ranks have been reflected in a shift in decision-making from the Commission to the Council of Ministers (and on a day-to-day basis the Committee of Permanent Representatives) where member states feel that their views can be put more effectively. The Commission negotiates on the basis of 'mandates' which are drawn up by the Council of Ministers. Since 1977, these mandates have been particularly tight, limiting the margin for independent initiative by the Commission. This has been largely on British and French instigation. At the same time, Community level negotiations have been supplemented by bilateral discussions between member states and third parties. Thus both France and Britain have invoked Article XIX of the GATT against third parties where they felt that the EEC was too slow or unwilling to act. West Germany has had a series of talks with the East German government in efforts to stem abuses of the trade agreement between the two where textiles are concerned. In April 1981, Lord Carrington, the British Foreign Secretary, is reported to have put textile discussions 'at the top of his agenda' in a visit to Portugal, in an attempt to negotiate voluntary limits of Portuguese clothing sales to the UK.[8]

International pressures

The EEC's attitude to the developing countries is clearly conditioned by its relations with other textile producers over which it has less influence. The American dimension of EEC textile policy has been crucial. It has been affected by broader political factors, including concern for the stability of the western alliance at a time of uncertainty over Iran and Afghanistan. EEC textile policy towards the USA has become increasingly strong in tone of voice, but has not produced the controls for which industrial groups hoped. The fear of trade retaliation, and wider political factors, have restrained European governments. Similarly, while negotiations with the northern Mediterranean countries are separate from those with developing states, they have a direct bearing on each other. The EEC has Association agreements with the main Mediterranean textile suppliers, and these limit the kinds of control which can be enforced against their imports. Portugal, Greece, and Spain all invested in textiles in expectation that both before and after their accession to the Community they would enjoy a substantial advantage in clothing and textile products. While some authorities have suggested that the enlargement of the EEC will have little effect on developing country exports to Europe,[9] there has been growing evidence that this view is optimistic.

The developing countries have been trying to strengthen their negotiating position. This has never been easy to do, given their differing interests and their severe want of diplomatic and technical resources for effective policy coordination. The cotton producers began to act in a concerted way in the 1977 talks, and planned to build on this in the 1981 MFA negotiations. In 1980, Indonesia restricted imports from Britain in retaliation for the way in which it was implementing MFA rules against

Indonesian goods. This example has been seized on eagerly by other developing states. Clearly only a few have the means to make such sanctions work, and it is much more difficult for developing states to impose retaliation on the EEC as a whole than it is to attack one member. But, in part, the test concerns the degree of unity obtainable in the Third World camp. At their meeting in Tunis in Spring 1981, the foreign ministers of the Arab League offered active support for Arab countries in negotiations on textiles with the EEC.

Third World unity will be severely tested during the negotiations on MFA III and the related bilateral agreements of 1981 and 1982. In April 1981, the Commission formulated its views.[10] It called for a renewal of the MFA with a shift in favour of the poorest producers at the expense of the larger newly industrialising producers. It rejected the idea of restrictions on developed country exports into the EEC, but advocated new and tighter measures to oversee imports from preferential countries (Lomé, Mediterranean and Associate countries). And it called for a reappraisal of outward processing to develop it as a part of an industrial co-operation strategy with the Third World. In mid-July 1981, the Council of foreign ministers approved a negotiating mandate for the talks, due to open in the early autumn, which took the Commission proposals as a basis but made them tougher in certain ways at the demand of France, Britain, Belgium and Italy.[11] The negotiating brief included a recession clause to be added to the MFA, to enable the EEC to make absolute cuts in imports if EEC domestic markets decline further as a result of recession (as at present seems likely). It was also suggested that the EEC should discriminate against countries which themselves operated trade restrictions on industrial goods from the Community. Both of these ideas have in the past been dismissed by the Commission as difficult if not impossible to implement. Their inclusion in the negotiating brief indicates that the EEC will be taking a very tough stand.

The future of textile and clothing arrangements between the EEC and the Third World is therefore uncertain. But the outcome of the MFA negotiations will be the result of structural, market and corporatist pressures, together with the dispositions habitually worn into powerful states, rather than of purely economic arguments. While no one in the EEC has any intention of harming the developing countries as a deliberate action, the net effect of EEC internal policy-making, political and industrial perceptions, and of external pressures, is to produce a policy which has profound and generally harmful effects on ldc producers. Even those countries which enjoy larger quotas or EEC investment, have the shape of their industries' development determined by outside control. Those which lack quotas find it hard to break into the market and these countries include some of the poorest and smallest developing countries. EEC trade policies have a much greater effect in limiting industrial development in the Third World than the EEC's aid policy, with limited funds, can possibly have in fostering it.

Notes

1 European Commission, *The European Community's Textile Trade* 44/81 EEC Commission, Brussels, 1981. Appendix A.
2 United Nations, *UN Yearbook of International Trade Statistics* Vol. 2, United Nations, New York, 1979. pp. 123–9.
3 European Commission, *Report on the Operation of the MFA* COM (80), Brussels, EEC Commission, October 1980. 438 final.
4 J. de la Torre, 'Decline and adjustment: public intervention strategies in the European clothing industries', mimeo paper, INSEAD, Fontainebleau, July 1980.
5 Two Gesamtextil reports are available from them at 6000 Frankfurt am Main 70, Schaumainkai 87.
6 See also Chris Farrands, 'External relations: textile politics and the MFA', in Wallace, Wallace and Webb (eds) *Policy Making in the European Communities*, revised 2nd edition, forthcoming, Wiley.
7 For more details see ibid.
8 *Daily Telegraph*, 27 April 1981.
9 N. Kim, *The Second Enlargement of the EEC: Implications for Korea, Taiwan, Hong Kong and Singapore*, Seoul, Centre for Economic Research, 1979.
10 European Commission, 1981, op. cit.
11 *Financial Times*, 14 July 1981.

7

The Multifibre Arrangement and Outward Processing: the Case of Morocco and Tunisia

Susan Joekes

As noted in Chapter 6, there are loopholes in the Multifibre Arrangement (MFA) that allow preferential access to clothing that has been 'outward processed'. It provides therefore some degree of stimulus for ldc clothing industries to develop in a close relationship with firms based in the industrialised countries, instead of on a more autonomous basis. Morocco and Tunisia have both developed important clothing industries oriented towards exports, primarily to the EEC, but with significant differences between them in the role of foreign private capital and outward processing. This chapter examines the experience of these two countries and the insights that they provide on the positive and negative features of outward processing at a time of growing protectionism.

The Maghreb and the EEC

All three Maghreb states (Morocco, Tunisia and Algeria) have associate status with the EEC, but because of the importance of oil in Algeria's exports the story of clothing concerns only Morocco and Tunisia. The details of Morocco and Tunisia's trade agreements with the EEC are given in *Survey 1* Chapter 4, and figures on aggregate trade flows are given in the Statistical Appendix. One of the central principles of the commercial arrangements between the EEC and both countries introduced in 1970 was the granting of duty free access for industrial exports satisfying the Community rules of origin, ie for products manufactured more or less in their entirety in the exporting country or else with materials made in the EEC. Table 7.1 shows the composition and share of manufactured products in total EEC imports from the Maghreb countries. Industrial exports consist mainly of 'textiles, mainly clothing'.

Table 7.1 *Broad commodity composition of Moroccan and Tunisian exports to EEC 1970–79 (million Ecu)*

	Morocco			*Tunisia*		
	Agricultural Products	*Industrial Products*	*Total*	*Agricultural Products*	*Industrial Products*	*Total*
1970	237.4	161.4	398.8	38.9	79.4	118.3
1971	222.5	160.0	382.5	45.2	89.2	134.4
1972	259.1	171.6	430.7	67.5	124.5	192.0
1973	357.7	224.0	581.7	95.4	95.8	191.2
1974	334.4	576.5	910.9	136.1	287.5	423.6
1975	316.6	489.3	805.9	84.0	273.3	357.3
1976	353.6	425.9	779.5	75.8	332.8	408.6
1977	355.1	479.2	834.3	114.8	437.4	552.2
1978	356.0	484.8	840.8	99.6	465.6	565.2
1979	387.6	624.8	1 012.4	140.0	650.3	790.3

Source: EEC Commission.

Exports of clothing from Morocco and Tunisia have increased extremely rapidly during the 1970s.

The development of the textile industry

Both Morocco and Tunisia pursued a strategy of import substituting, protected industrialisation from independence in 1956 through the 1960s. During this period the textile industry was established in Tunisia and considerably expanded in Morocco (the bigger country, where more industrialisation had taken place under the French). In each case a broadly based textile industry was developed, mainly through public investment in Tunisia, almost entirely with local private capital in Morocco. Production covered the whole range of textile operations from spinning and weaving to production of finished clothing. By the end of the decade it was in both places the largest national industry in terms of output and employment, and each country was approaching self-sufficiency in textiles. The only route for significant further expansion lay in production for foreign markets. Association with the EEC at this time, with its provision for duty free access for manufactures, therefore came opportunely, and continued, very rapid, expansion of textile production since then has largely been based on export to the European market. Expansion in this phase has been concentrated on clothing, rather than production of yarn or fabric or other textile products.[1]

Despite their historical similarities the two clothing industries nowadays differ in two important and probably interconnected respects. The shares of both foreign capital and outward processing business are

What is outward processing?

'Outward processing' refers to the situation where a trader sends materials to another country to be made up and imported back on his own account. It is almost, but not quite, synonymous with international sub-contracting. Although there is no standard definition of international sub-contracting, it is generally reckoned to include the delegation of supply of components to an essentially centralised manufacturing process, whereas outward processing refers to the delegation to another enterprise of the performance of certain stages of fabrication – generally actual assembly – of the main product itself. Outward processing also necessarily refers to the transfer of the product at different stages of completion out and back across national boundaries (or in this case the EEC bloc boundary), while international sub-contracting is sometimes held to include arrangements between firms of different national ownership situated in the same country. The contractual relationship between the firm which organises the outward processing (the EEC principal) and the Maghrebi firm performing the operation (the contractor) entails the following:

1 part or all of the contractor's production capacity is committed in advance to the principal for a predetermined period for production of whatever goods (or performance of whatever feasible processes) the principal may determine;
2 the principal supplies the designs and main inputs (primarily in this case, the fabric, cut or uncut, but sometimes also other materials, such as thread, fastenings, trimmings, labels and packaging materials). These materials remain in effect the principal's property, even if a paper transaction is entered in the contractor's books. The contractor's obligation is to the principal only; the contractor has nothing to do with marketing the product.
3 As a consequence of this the principal carries ultimate responsibility for quality control and so supplies technical assistance to improve production methods as well as quality controls.
4 There is no necessary equity link between the parties.

The incidence of outward processing is not limited to clothing although this is the archetypal case or to the despatch of materials to low-wage countries, though again this is typical. Its main growth has been in the past twenty years. In the USA and West Germany outward processed imports from ldcs increased at annual rates of 60 % and 36 % respectively over the period 1966–72, much faster than the increase in manufactured imports as a whole from the same countries; by 1972, 22 % of USA and 10 % of German ldc imports were of this type. All the signs are that this expansion has continued since and that present shares are larger in both the main productive activities concerned, electronics (in the case of the USA) and clothing (in Europe). Outward processing of clothing is very widespread, concentrated perhaps in the Far East but spreading in the Maghreb, Latin America, the Caribbean, South Asia and East and Southern Europe.

> At the commissioning end there are few reliable estimates of the importance of outward processed products in total clothing imports of industrialised countries but, for example, in the USA outward processed clothes, which constituted 10.3 % of total ldc clothing imports in 1974 increased in value by 70 % in the succeeding four year period; and by 1978 43 supplying countries were involved. In West Germany the share of outward processed clothing in ldc clothing imports reached 17 % in 1974 and 1975 (though it has slipped back a little since), and in the Netherlands it reached 20 % in 1975.

considerably higher in Tunisia than in Morocco. Soon after the 1970 EEC association agreements, Morocco and Tunisia introduced similar fiscal and administrative measures designed to provide incentives for investment in exporting activities and to attract foreign capital which were indicative of a shift towards a (selectively) export-oriented industrialisation strategy.[2] Tunisia was much more successful than Morocco in the latter aim. More than three-quarters of new jobs in the clothing industry in Tunisia in the period 1973–76 were in majority foreign-owned firms[3] but in Morocco very little new foreign capital was invested in clothing.[4] The reasons for the different experiences of the two countries are obscure. Foreign investors enjoy slightly more favourable conditions in Tunisia, but hardly sufficient according to the formal regulations to explain the extent of the difference. The explanation perhaps lies in the perception of greater political instability and the general policy of majority local ownership in joint ventures in Morocco, even though there is nominal exemption from the latter requirement for exporting firms.

The second difference between the two countries is that in Tunisia production of clothing for export is almost entirely outward processed, whereas in Morocco it is only around one-third of the total.[5] The types of principal involved in outward processing can be classified according to their nationality and the nature of their business. The firms involved are almost exclusively French, German, Dutch and Belgian. In Morocco, French principals predominate, with German firms closing up behind. In Tunisia, Dutch and German firms seem to be dominant. British firms are conspicuous by their absence in both places. The types of firms range from brand name and wholesale manufacturers (who do not market their products under any one label), to non-manufacturing wholesalers, mail order firms and chain and department stores. Manufacturers tend to set up more fully integrated operations with their contractors than non-manufacturers, though department stores and mail order stores have their own technical production staff who are fully capable of supervising and directing outward processing operations. Firms which are not themselves otherwise directly involved in production tend to commission simpler types of garments, and the independent contractor has greater scope for offering his own designs. In such cases the dividing line between outward processing and bulk supply contracts can become rather weak. However the bulk of outward processing in the full sense is organised by firms which are themselves manufacturers. Supervision of the contractor's production operations is closest and the amount of technical assistance provided is most complete for high quality, high fashion branded garments.

The types of contractor involved in Morocco and Tunisia can be classified according to national ownership and the types of garment produced. When a contractor has an equity link with the principals – which is the norm in Tunisia, but rare in Morocco – the outward processing relationship is stable and enduring and the contractor is likely to place his whole production capacity at the disposal of the principal. In other cases the contractor is likely to have two or three principals for whom work is done at any time under short or medium-term contracts of one to three years and may well experience a considerable rate of turnover among his principals. The nominal term of the contract is not of much significance because the contract can be easily broken off by the principal who faces no effective sanction and does not compensate the contractor, as some independent Moroccan clothing firms discovered in 1980.[6]

The extent of outward processing is much more common in one of the two main sub-branches of the clothing industry, tailored goods, than in the other, knitted goods. This is primarily because the chain of vertically integrated operations undertaken by the manufacturer is longer in the case of knitted goods production than in tailored goods production. The knitted goods producer buys in yarn (rather than knitted fabric) and the final garment is more or less knitted to shape on programmable looms, with minimal cutting and making up operations in the final stages. Tailored goods production on the other hand involves buying in fabric which is cut into a large number of separate pieces for each garment whose subsequent assembly constitutes an intricate making up process. Outward processing hinges on the supply of the major input and is clearly more suited to the latter process. The different ranges of garments exported from Morocco and Tunisia reflect this distinction.[7]

The motives of the principals in setting up outward processing arrangements are straightforward: it is done to save labour costs in order to maintain competitiveness in the final product price. The production of clothing remains a relatively highly labour intensive process in which labour costs are crucial. Labour costs are estimated to account for 27 % of total production costs on average in North America and from 28 % to 53 % of total costs in Europe.[8] Variations in national labour costs are difficult to measure but one estimate[9] is that wages in low cost countries ranged in 1977 from 9 % of the US level in South Korea to around 20 % in Brazil and Hong Kong and 30–40 % in southern European countries outside the EEC. Information is unfortunately not available on this score for Morocco and Tunisia, but wage levels are likely to be somewhat below the level of other Mediterranean countries outside the EEC.[10] Inside the EEC, the richer countries (Germany, Denmark, Belgium and the Netherlands) have higher wage rates than the USA (at about 130 %) while France (at 90 %) is slightly below the USA level and the UK (at 50 %) is very much below. The disparity between the wage level in the richer European countries and in low-cost countries is as great or greater than the difference from the USA level, but considerably less – in some cases negligible – as far as the UK is concerned. This suggests that the incentive to arrange outward processing is higher for the richer European countries than even in the American case, but very slight, or even non-existent, for the UK.[11] This hierarchy tallies with the national identities of foreign principals operating in the Maghreb. International relocation of parts of clothing production to take advantage of these wide wage differentials is made possible by favourable technological conditions and low international transportation costs. Proximity is an advantage and this probably explains the recent growth of outward processing for the European market in Eastern Europe and in the countries bordering the Mediterranean.

In Tunisia the majority of contractors are subsidiaries of foreign companies set up expressly to do outward processing for European principals. In Morocco on the other hand most contractors are wholly locally owned. The main reason why independent firms undertake outward processing is that the fabric is supplied by the principal. The high cost, poor quality and unreliability of supplies of locally made cloth are standing complaints among Maghreb clothing manufacturers.[12] The cash flow problems of clothing production are largely relieved by outward processing. Many firms also welcome the close involvement of the foreign firm in production and even encourage it because they see in it a way of shifting the responsibility for quality control onto the foreign firm; the maintenance of consistent standards is crucial and failure jeopardises the ability to make and the profitability of particular deals. Some Moroccan employers claim that by applying the principal's methods of work organisation throughout the plant they are able to improve the profitability of their local operations. Lastly employers recognise the benefits of the relatively long production runs which a contractual relationship brings.

Outward processing and protectionism

In addition to these private gains to both sides, outward processing has been encouraged by the organisation of EEC protection to the domestic clothing industry. The principals in the EEC have an interest in moderating restrictions on their trade and, probably for this reason, the MFA accords preferences to outward processed imports over imports produced wholly in ldcs.

Like other ldcs, Morocco and Tunisia found their clothing exports limited by MFA II, despite the formal provision of duty free access to the EEC for manufactured goods incorporated in their association agreements. However, they fared rather better than some ldcs. Because of their preferential trading status they were required to adopt voluntary export restraints (so as not to clash with the letter of their trading agreements) under the threat of unilateral imposition by the Community of the safeguard clause which allows limitation of 'disruptive' imports. The burden of observing this type of restraint lies in principle with the authorities of the exporting country, though imports were also monitored in the importing country. Moreover, the Mediterranean countries were favoured with a higher than average growth ceiling.

Despite similar treatment, Morocco and Tunisia fared very differently (see Table 7.2). Morocco's exports actually declined in current value in 1977. In both 1977 and 1978 it failed to fulfill its MFA quota: in 1978 the average rate of fulfilment in all products except one was about 33 %.[13] By contrast, Tunisia managed to double its exports in 1977 and to increase them again, by 42 %, in the following year, by which time its exports were three times the Moroccan amount in value terms. Several factors may have contributed to this difference but it seems likely that two important influences were the higher levels of outward processing in Tunisia and the much higher levels of private investment by EEC firms in the outward processing sector. Outward processed products were generally subject to the MFA restrictions at only half rate in 1977 and 1978, and at one-third the rate in 1979–81,[14] although in practice not all national members of the EEC recognise the distinction: the UK gives no concession on this point, but France and West Germany do, and are the most important markets for the Maghreb countries. Thus, two or three pieces of outward processed clothing are reckoned as the equivalent of one non-outward processed garment – which effectively doubles or triples the quantity limit. Moroccan officials and producers ascribe the poor performance in 1977 to the disruption of normal importing channels. It is likely that arms-length transactions were much more severely affected by uncertainty about the new rules than were outward processing transactions

Table 7.2 *Exports to EEC[a] of clothing (SITC 841) from Morocco and Tunisia* ($'000)

	1970	*1975*	*1976*	*1977*	*1978*
Morocco	—[b]	43 438	58 167	58 093	65 754
Tunisia	1 000	44 667	70 406	140 273	199 561

a Approximately equal to total clothing exports.
b Not available, but negligible quantity.

Source: *UN Yearbook of International Trade Statistics*

(especially those involving foreign private investment) where the principal would have had a strong interest in sorting out the regulations and making sure its goods got through.

Thus, by making full use of the loopholes and of links with EEC-based firms, Tunisia was able to avoid being adversely affected by MFA II. But a policy of systematically utilising outward processing backed by foreign investment long pre-dates the MFA. The reason for the initial adoption of outward processing as the mode for export production lies in the qualitative regulations of the EEC-Maghreb country commercial treaties, in particular the rules of origin. The quality and price of Moroccan and Tunisian cloth are in general uncompetitive internationally as a consequence of the development of small scale spinning and weaving capacity under protection in the immediate post-independence, import substituting period of industrialisation. The introduction of duty free access to the EEC for wholly locally made garments was therefore largely an empty concession. Had Maghrebi producers had the option of using the cheapest available imported fabric they might have been able to develop production of low cost, basic garments for the European market. But the need to use high quality, relatively expensive European fabric meant they had to move instead towards the production of garments in the medium to high quality range of the clothing market, which in addition was suitable for their small average size as producers[15] since 'fashion' garments of this type do not generally rely on long production runs. But to jump into production of relatively high quality goods in this way also necessarily required considerable technical assistance. The combination added up to a strong case for arrangements of the outward processing type. The reciprocity basis of the 1970 association agreements proved a reinforcing factor, since this required that EEC fabric be admitted duty free to the Maghreb countries. Such impetus to outward processing is likely to be strengthened by increasing protectionism that puts a premium on the political and practical support of principals in the EEC. The question that arises is whether such a mode of industrial development is desirable from the viewpoint of the ldcs.

The impact of outward processing on ldc development

Outward processing was encouraged by the Moroccan and Tunisian authorities in the expectation that it would provide particularly attractive conditions for foreign capital, it would enable technological expertise to be built up quickly, it would be employment-creating, and would be a means of penetrating the highly differentiated and volatile clothing market. How far have these objectives been achieved? The different success of the two countries shows that encouragement of outward processing is not in itself a sufficient incentive to attract foreign capital, although it may be that in sites which are favourably regarded by foreign investors for other reasons, the decision to commit funds is finalised if outward processing is facilitated by the local authorities.

Undoubtedly, technology transfer does take place under outward processing. But process rather than product technology is mostly what is entailed, and the technology is not of an advanced kind. More importantly, local build up of technological expertise will not serve the ultimate objective of improving the autonomous capacity to export clothing if the trend in outward processing continues because there will be few market opportunities for fully locally produced goods. Moreover, where foreign capital is involved (as in Tunisia) genuinely local technological capacity will be little affected unless limitations are set on the employment of expatriate personnel. The transfer of process technology should, for locally managed enterprises, improve the organisational capacity of local producers. But outward processing necessarily deprives management of the challenge, and opportunity, of exercising the complete range of entrepreneurial skills, by reducing the need for risk taking and for design and marketing of the product.

Outward processing sited in low-cost countries is done predominantly to take advantage of low wages in the labour intensive stages of a production process. Therefore, for a given value of output in a particular industry, the employment created is probably *greater* in outward processing than in local production of the product in its entirety. But in the clothing industry in Morocco and Tunisia, as in outward processing elsewhere, recruitment of workers to the new jobs is particularly selective. The new employees are predominantly women, usually young and unmarried.[16] This modifies the national benefits normally expected of employment creation. Because women's wages are lower than men's, the benefit in terms of labour income obtained from outward processing is less than normal, and of the order of 60 %. In the extreme case, retained labour income is almost the only benefit from outward processing which, if wholly foreign owned, will generate no income to local capital and contribute nothing to local technological capacity (all outward processing is normally exempt from corporate taxes and uses little or no supplies from local industry[17]). In such a case an adjustment to retained labour income of this magnitude has very considerable consequences for the assessment of overall benefit. Furthermore, the provision of jobs for women, which in both countries represents an almost unprecedented opportunity for female wage labour, technically has a greater effect in increasing the labour force participation than in reducing the number of unemployed. This increase in opportunity for women is, in many respects, attractive, particularly from a social perspective, but in terms of income distribution, the new women workers tend to be drawn from relatively well-off families. Hence the effect is not unambiguously beneficial, although undoubtedly many of the new jobs provide financial support for disadvantaged families, particularly those without any working adult male member.

Thus, while it is certainly true that outward processing is a way round difficult marketing problems for 'fashion' type clothing, and is of increasing value in an era of rising protectionism, the other side of the coin is that learning does not come without doing. The major disadvantage inherent in outward processing is that it cannot foster 'backward linkages', ie the development of local supplying industries, in this case upstream textile production and, after that, local capacity in sewing machinery manufacture. Moreover, it is clear that outward processing has failed to achieve many of the objectives set for it by the Moroccan and Tunisian authorities. It should be seen for what it is: a circumscribed and contingent means of generating some foreign exchange and labour income, but probably not an effective instrument of industrialisation.

Notes

1 Except in Morocco, where hand-knotted carpets are the single biggest export textile product. We exclude carpets entirely from the discussion; they are in any case an artisanal rather than an industrial product.

2 For details see OECD Development Centre, 'International subcontracting: the case of Tunisia', by M. Falise, *Industry and Technology Occasional Paper no 17*, 1977; and OECD Development Centre, 'International subcontracting: the case of Morocco', by C. Berthomieu and A. Hanaut, *Industry and Technology Occasional Paper no. 18*, 1977.

3 Tilburg University Development Research Institute, 'Export industry in Tunisia; Effects of a dependent development', Research Project on International Relations and Industrial Structures, *Occasional Papers no. 5*, 1979.

4 Probably less than 10% of all new textiles investment was foreign; some old foreign (French) capital remains from the colonial period. See S. Joekes, 'Women's jobs in Third World export manufacturing: the Moroccan clothing industry', *IDS Research Report*, forthcoming, 1981. In Tunisia 57% of total national industrial investment was foreign in 1979 (Tunisia API (Agence pour le Promotion des Investissements)), whereas in Morocco 15% of total national investment was foreign in 1977 (Citibank, *Investment Guide: Morocco*, Rabat, n.d. (1980)).

5 ILO, Report II, BNDE, Morocco, 1980, p. 17.

6 S. Joekes, 1981, op. cit.

7 Moroccan exports include more knitted goods in the total bundle (albeit still a modest share: 23% in 1978), while Tunisia concentrates on tailored clothes, in particular trousers, shirts, and bras.

8 ILO, Tripartite Technical Committee on Textiles, *Report I*, Geneva, 1980.

9 ibid.

10 Total production costs for clothing are said to be three times greater in continental Europe than in Tunisia, taking account of wage and productivity differentials and transport costs (OECD, Occasional Paper 17, 1977, op. cit.).

11 The situation of Italy is anomalous: it is an important site for outward processing, particularly for German principals.

12 Joekes 1981, op. cit and Tilburg University 1979, op. cit.
13 Ministere de la Commerce et de l'Industrie, *Colloque Nationale 'Industrie Textile'*, Rabat, Morocco, 1978.
14 EEC, *Accord de Co-operation CEE-Maroc*, Brussels, January 1980.
15 No Moroccan clothing firm has a workforce of more than 500.
16 Joekes 1981, op. cit, and Tilburg University 1979, op. cit.
17 National income data on foreign exchange earnings in outward processed activities are in general spurious and misleading. The total value of garments exported is recorded, which includes the value of imported (foreign owned) materials incorporated in them. Finger estimates that the net impact on developing countries' trade balances of outward processing activities is only about 10% of the nominal value. (J. M. Finger, 'Tariff provisions for offshore assembly and the exports of developing countries', *Economic Journal*, vol. 85, June 1975, p. 338 ff.)

Part 3

The Plight of the Least Developed Countries

8

The Least Developed Countries: A Role for the EEC

J. Verloren van Themaat

In September 1981 the UN convened a conference devoted to the problems of the least developed countries (lldcs) which, during the 1970s, saw their economic situation stagnate or deteriorate both absolutely and in relation to other developing countries (ldcs). This group, which now numbers 31 countries,[1] was first identified by the UN in 1971 and is defined to include those states that combine a very low per capita GNP, a low literacy rate, and an undeveloped industrial sector. As is explained in Chapter 9, the precise definition of categories of states like the lldcs is fraught with political innuendo. For this reason some EEC member states were lukewarm towards the conference, which was also criticised by those who believe that concentration on the problems of the lldcs is divisive and diverts attention from the structural problems affecting the Third World as a whole.

Nonetheless, there are some good reasons in analysing the plight of the lldcs. First, despite the contentious nature of the precise classification, the economic performance of the group's members during the 1970s was strikingly similar and depressingly poor (see Table 8.1). Second, this poor performance was due not only to domestic factors but also to the lldcs' position in the international economic system and hence on their commercial and financial links with the industrialised countries. Third, their poor performance has occurred despite an increase in the aid committed to them and so brings into question the true impact of aid. Finally, it is particularly appropriate for this *Survey* to focus upon the lldcs because the EEC is their most important partner for aid and trade. 21 of the 31 members of the group belong to the Lomé Convention (see *Survey 1*, Chapter 3), and therefore receive preferential treatment on trade and priority on aid. This chapter begins with an analysis of the recent economic performance of the lldcs. On the basis of this analysis, it assesses the relevance of the prescriptions put before the UN conference, and proposes a new policy for the EEC and the other developed countries.

Table 8.1 *Basic indicators for least developed countries as compared with all developing countries and developed countries*

		All least developed countries	*All developing countries*	*Socialist countries of Eastern Europe*	*Developed market economy countries*
Population (millions)	1979	267.9	2164.6	375.7	780.5
Per cent of labour force in agriculture	1979	82	59	21	9
GDP per capita annual average growth rates (per cent)	1960–1979	0.7	2.9	5.4[a]	3.4
GDP, $ per capita of which:	1978	201	661	3681	7922
Agricultural output	1978	94	119	–	317
Manufacturing output	1978	18	126	–	2297
Exports, $ per capita	1979	20.0	103.7[b]	362.3	1378.4
Concessional assistance $ per capita	1979	18.9	13.0[b]		
Energy Consumption per capita (kg of coal equivalent)	1978	53	449	5477	6362
Health Physicians per 100 000 population	1977[c]	5.9	10.3	257.7	159.5
Education Secondary school enrolment ratio (per cent)	1977[c]	12	28	72	86

[a] Net material product.
[b] Excluding major petroleum exporters.
[c] Or latest year available.

Source: UNCTAD secretariat based on data from the United Nations Statistical Office, FAO, UNESCO, OECD/DAC and World Bank.

The worsening economic position of the lldcs

The economic growth of the lldcs as a group stagnated during the 1970s (their GDP per capita grew by only 0.8 % p.a. 1970–78) and for ten the per capita growth was negative (Cape Verde, C.A.R., Chad, Comoros, Ethiopia, Laos, Lesotho, Mali, Uganda and Upper Volta). Food production increased at only 1.9 % p.a. in the same period, well below the populatión growth of 2.4 %, and the average for all developing countries of 3.0 %. Agricultural productivity is probably much lower than in other ldcs. Investment growth per year fell from 6.4 % p.a. in the 1960s to only

2.6 % in the 1970s. The purchasing power of the lldcs' exports has decreased by 1.9 % p.a. 1970–78, compared with an increase of 4.2 % p.a. for the developing countries as a whole. Moreover, the volume of imports increased by 3.9 % p.a. 1970–78, resulting in an ever increasing current account deficit. As far as social indicators are concerned, there have been increases in the number of illiterates, and in migration.

Internal or external factors?

The introduction of the concept of the least developed countries has tended to focus attention on the domestic characteristics of the lldcs, and on common characteristics *within* the group, such as the fact that 15 of the 31 are landlocked, their climate (Sahel), their low agricultural productivity, their high illiteracy percentages (80 % of the population over 15 years), their low level of industrialisation (9 % of GDP in 1978), their low life-expectancy (45 years).

These are indeed important indicators of slow economic progress. And the UN Programme of Action for the lldcs prepared for the 1981 conference rightly proposes a strong attack on these problems. But they do not indicate the whole picture. Also important is the way in which these countries are integrated into the world economic system. There appear to be tendencies inherent in the international economic system which make these countries increasingly vulnerable, which distort their internal allocation of production factors and deprive them of the possibility of a balanced and self-sustained economic growth. Four examples illustrate this tendency. In the area of food, the relationship between production for domestic consumption and for export is of crucial importance. The balance between them has been influenced strongly by external factors and price relationships as well as by domestic factors. It is striking that the exports of countries in which hunger is such a problem are dominated by food products. In 1977, 52 % (by value) of lldc exports consisted of food products (most notably coffee), while for 10 countries the proportion exceeded 75 %. In the area of trade generally, it is important to note not only that the trade of the lldcs has been growing more slowly than that of the developing countries as a whole (10 % p.a. against 21 % p.a. 1970–78), but also that their terms of trade have deteriorated as a result of external factors. In terms of manpower, the lldcs are seeing their labour attracted to better paid jobs not just in the developed countries but increasingly in the faster growing developing countries: the Arab OPEC countries form a magnet for labour from the two Yemens, Sudan, Ethiopia and Somalia; Senegal for the Gambia; Ivory Coast for Upper Volta, Mali and Niger; Kenya for Uganda and Tanzania. Hence the lldcs' shortages of trained manpower are not only a result of a poor internal education system. There has probably been a similar attraction of domestic capital away from lldcs towards their faster growing neighbours. This external pull is one of the reasons why domestic investment in lldcs grew very slowly in the 1970s (2.6 % p.a. 1970–78 as against 6.4 % p.a. in 1960–70). Moreover, direct foreign investment has been very low in the lldcs ($0.30 per caput in 1977) and has been increasing more slowly than population.

External assistance

One of the few areas in which the position of the lldcs has been clearly 'improving' is in the amount of external assistance they receive. Aid increased from $900 million in 1970 to $4 billion in 1978 and $5.1 billion in 1979. Even in constant dollars this is almost a doubling. Also per capita external assistance has increased at constant prices from $10.6 in 1972 to $15.7 in 1978. The share of aid going to the least developed has increased over the decade, especially from the DAC countries, although this relative growth has stagnated somewhat since 1975. Among the OECD countries, most of the EEC states and the Scandinavian countries have devoted a considerably larger share of their concessional assistance to the least developed than have the other members, notably the USA and Japan (see Table 8.2 and 8.3).

Table 8.2 *Share of lldcs in ODA flows from individual DAC members* (percentage, 1978)

Belgium	24
Denmark	39
France	9
W. Germany	23
Italy	40
Netherlands	27
UK	23
Australia	7
Canada	26
Finland	46
Japan	14
Norway	42
Sweden	35
USA	14
OECD average	18

Table 8.3 *Share of lldcs in concessional loans and grants to all ldcs*

	1965–68	*1972*	*1975*	*1976*	*1977*	*1978*
Total	11.8	13.4	19.2	17.7	18.6	19.5
OECD	11.3	12.2	20.4	18.2	19.2	20.9
OPEC	—	—	13.1	14.4	16.6	11.7
E. Europe	17.0	29.2	38.0	37.0	14.9	16.0

Source: OECD DAC Secretariat.

There are a number of possible reasons for this increased share of aid going to the least developed. It can be partly explained by popular pressure in the donor countries to give more aid to the poorest countries, and by the sudden interest in the Sahel countries, resulting from the drought. There are also less humanitarian explanations. The most important shift in aid patterns to lldcs took place in 1975, one year after the oil crisis (see Table 8.3). There was a clear wish among the European countries to improve their relations with the Arab world, and one way to do this was to increase aid to poor Arab or Moslem countries. A generous aid-giving country like the Netherlands, for example, increased its aid to two Arab lldcs (Yemen and Sudan) dramatically following the Arab oil boycott. Table 8.4 shows the proportion of aid disbursed by OECD

Table 8.4 *OECD disbursed aid to OPEC-linked lldcs and other lldcs*

OPEC-linked lldcs	*1974*	*1975*	*Percentage increase*
Afghanistan	16.9	32.6	92
Bangladesh	344.3	703.9	104
Benin	18.5	29.1	57
C.A.R.	18.6	33.3	79
Chad (1973/74)	26.4	37.9	43
Mali (1973/74)	34.9	60.2	72
Niger (1973/74)	42.1	82.6	96
Somalia	7.3	23.3	219
Sudan	33.2	60.2	81
Upper Volta (1973/74)	34.7	50.2	45
Yemen, A.R.	27.4	15.0	45
Other lldcs			
Botswana	29.9	38.6	29
Burundi	18.7	26.4	41
Comoros	27.1	17.5	−35
Ethiopia	79.8	73.1	−8
Gambia	3.7	3.6	−3
Guinea	6.7	3.5	−18
Haiti	9.4	24.8	164
Laos	57.3	32.6	−43
Lesotho	12.6	14.7	17
Malawi	30.5	47.1	54
Nepal	20.5	28.6	39
Rwanda	26.2	31.6	21
Samoa	4.3	8.8	104
Tanzania	140.2	234.8	67
Uganda	6.8	4.5	−33
Yemen, Dem.	5.0	6.1	22

Note: No figures available for Bhutan, Maldives and Cape Verde.

Source: UNCTAD.

countries to OPEC-linked lldcs and to other lldcs, and shows that the aid increase to the first group following the first oil crisis has been much more substantial than to the second group. Europe has played more forcefully this card of establishing links with the Arab world than the USA or Japan.

The increasing aid flow to the least developed has had important effects on the receiving economies which go far beyond the intended objectives of increased exports, increased food production, better infrastructure, improved health conditions, etc. Because of their weakening external position the lldcs have become increasingly dependent on aid for the financing of their imports. In 1979, aid financed almost 50 % of the total imports of the lldcs, a dramatic increase from 1970, when concessional assistance only financed 30 % of imports. This trend has obvious policy implications for the lldc governments. If they want to maintain their import level, they have to stay on good terms with their aid donors. These very important and growing financial flows have also influenced the role of the state in the lldcs. Often they have reinforced centralising tendencies within national bureaucratic structures. The shift of their financial resource base from internal sources to external aid sources has been paralleled by a shift in political power balances within governments, and between governments and the private sector. It has had a tendency to make governments more sensitive and responsive to external relations, sometimes to the detriment of domestic needs. In addition, and perhaps less obviously, the donors have used their financial power quite considerably to influence in a detailed way how these flows are spent, and as intended or unintended leverage on the related economic policies of the recipients. Arguably the level of influence per dollar of aid is considerably higher in the least developed than in other developing countries. Firstly, this is because more aid is given on a project basis than in other developing countries. Projects are usually accompanied by close donor supervision of feasibility, modalities of execution, tendering procedures, origin of the procurement, etc. Secondly, because a substantial amount of technical assistance accompanies project aid. Thirdly, because the greater dependence on donor finance gives the recipient countries less negotiation power and therefore creates a greater influence per dollar of aid.

In most lldcs almost the entire government investment budget is financed by external aid. As a result, this budget is geared towards the requirements of the international aid mechanism. Investments are project-oriented. Their size is linked to aid possibilities and the conditions of individual donors or consortia. Projects tend to be large, despite all intentions to the contrary of the donors, because of the donors' limited administrative capacity for handling many small projects and because of the recipient tendency of 'overasking'. They are heavily foreign exchange-oriented. Paradoxically, even when they claim to support self-reliance, most foreign financed projects effectively integrate domestic economic, institutional and political forces into the world economy and make them dependent upon the latter. Although nobody would deny the need to co-ordinate foreign aid, the form which it has taken through institutions like the World Bank Consortia, Club de Sahel, etc., has been foreign dominated. The proposal to create a special UN institution for the lldcs would further reinforce this tendency.

The arguments used in Europe and other donor countries for heavy influence on aid in the lldcs boils down to: the need to account to their tax payers; the fact that the success of aid projects is also in the interests of the donors, or mankind generally as in the case of environmental, anti-desertification projects; the alleged low absorptive capacity of the lldcs. This last argument justifies some further examination. Although nobody would deny that there often is a lack of know-how in many lldcs, it does not necessarily justify the kind of involvement that the donors desire. It is not very logical to assume that while the lldcs were perfectly able to absorb their export earnings when their terms of trade were better, they are now not able to absorb the equivalent of their lost export earning capacity which they receive as aid! Secondly, as the OECD DAC secretariat has pointed out: 'It appears that a good part of the "limitation" on absorptive capacity is artificially engendered by development assistance agencies.'[2] The project approach is in itself very manpower and management intensive, usually involving extremely complicated administrative and follow-up procedures. Aid may have encouraged the brain drain of the educated and has probably strengthened the centralising tendency of governments to the detriment of the absorptive capacity of the rural areas.

Extremely slow economic progress, combined with continuous rising expectations of the newly educated elites has led to increasing political pressures and to a search for (sometimes drastic) alternatives. It is not surprising that a significant number of lldc governments are now, to varying degrees, anti-imperialist and anti-western. They include 12 countries, or almost 40 % of the total.[3] Many of these governments have turned to non-western powers for support, even where the latter provide less external assistance than do the OECD countries. This provides another political reason for increased European interest in the lldcs which appear to be more volatile in their political alliances and constitute a 'security risk' in the eyes of Europe.

The EEC and the least developed

The EEC is the most important economic partner of the least developed. It is their main trade partner, and also their main aid partner. For the 21 lldcs which are part of the Lomé Convention, 50–60 % of their imports are provided by the EEC and 40–50 % of their exports go to the EEC (see Table 8.5). Disbursed OECD bilateral aid to lldcs totalled $2.1 billion in 1978, and more than half of this ($1.2 billion) came from the EEC

Table 8.5 *Lldcs in ACP group trade with EEC and the world (1978)*

	Total Imports (in $ mn)	Of which: EEC in per cent	Total Exports (in $ mn)	Of which: EEC in per cent	*Main commodity groups of exports* (percentage) Food		Raw Materials		Manufacturing Production	
					EEC	World	EEC	World	EEC	World
Benin	267	59	26	50	44	26	52	51	3	18
Botswana	371	3	233	8	–	–	–	–	–	–
Burundi	58[c]	57	90	36	87	93	13	6	0	1
Cape Verde	36[c]	1	2	0	–	–	–	–	–	–
C.A.R.	85	73	107	70	52	42	29	33	19	23
Chad	192	54	102	20	–	19	96	68	2	2
Comoros	16[d]	43	9	66	59	–	–	–	–	–
Ethiopia	518	41	305	23	50[a]	57	48	37	1	3
Gambia	100	45	40	75	11[b]	11	89	87	0	–
Guinea	234	68	293	41	–	–	–	–	–	–
Lesotho	206[c]	1	17	2	–	–	–	–	–	–
Malawi	339	30	179	67	88	58	11	7	1	6
Mali	206	50	94	65	4	24	95	74	0	1
Niger	346	61	158	83	1	25	97	72	1	2
Rwanda	103[c]	48	70	13	–	–	–	–	–	–
Somalia	241	56	106	8	74	87	24	10	0	2
Sudan	1078	45	611	33	7	6	90	89	2	1
Tanzania	1117	52	457	50	75	60	11	26	12	9
Uganda	307	48	367	36	87	90	8	7	5	2
Upper Volta	209	61	55	47	6	43	88	51	6	6

Source: Eurostat. [a] 1974. [b] 1975. [c] 1976. [d] 1977.

member states' bilateral programmes. A substantial part of the European Development Fund aid goes to the lldcs among the ACP countries – 35 % of the total $266 million disbursed in 1978. Furthermore Stabex tends to favour these countries – 56 % of the disbursement in 1979.

It is clear therefore that the foregoing analysis has particular relevance for the EEC. The EEC serves as a major instrument integrating these countries into the world economy through its trade and aid relations, with all of the positive and negative implications that this has. Despite this importance, the EEC has been ambivalent about its relations with the lldcs. The perceived advantages to it, as outlined above, of increasing its aid to the lldcs has had to be set against other considerations: the opportunity cost of the resources involved, the relative insignificance of the lldcs in economic terms, and the often low short-term economic rate of return of aid to lldcs. Moreover, some member states have been lukewarm towards the concept of a special lldc group. Of the EEC member states, France has shown most interest in the geo-political advantages of supporting lldcs, and has been influenced, no doubt, by the fact that a great number of lldcs are former French colonies. It may therefore be more prepared than the others to create new facilities although it has not done so in the past (see Table 8.2). Thus far it may have demonstrated its geo-political interest more in the fields of military support and cultural relations than in the field of economic aid.

Since the UN created the group of the least developed in 1969, it has not really been able to solve the dilemmas mentioned above. When, in 1969, the UN Committee for Development Planning formulated for the first time the criteria which would differentiate the lldcs from all other ldcs by their sheer poverty, its objective was not to create a political group, to promote in any other way a cohesiveness between these countries, or to find an alternative strategy for them. The objective was purely and simply to try to get a large share of aid from the international donor community. UNCTADs III (1972), IV (1976), and V (1980) formulated increasingly detailed recommendations on the nature of these aid requirements, and on a number of secondary objectives. The deteriorating economic position of the lldcs during the 1970s greatly contributed to this more urgent appeal to the international community and culminated in a Programme of Action for the Least Developed Countries (UNCTAD V (122)) and the specially convened UN conference of September 1981.

The purpose of the Programme of Action is to expand greatly assistance to the lldcs, firstly 'for projects for the provision of the most pressing social needs' and secondly, to give assistance in 'transforming these economies towards self-sustained development, and enabling them to provide at least internationally accepted minimum standards of nutrition, health, transport and communications, housing and education as well as job opportunities to all their citizens, and particularly both rural and urban poor'. In short, the programme is heavily oriented towards more aid for a basic needs approach. However, in addition, attention is asked for better access of their exports via an even more preferred status within the Generalised System of Preferences (see Chapter 5) and for an improvement and extension of the transfer of technology. But generally rather little is said on this transformation to self-sustained economic development. A basic needs approach as such does not necessarily decrease their external dependence and their vulnerability to outside forces. On the contrary it could transform the lldcs even more into charity receivers, the aid donors having an even greater say in how the charity will be distributed.

What the lldcs need most are measures designed to change their structural relations with the outside world. In the field of trade this could mean special measures from the developed countries to increase their export earnings by giving price subsidies or long-term contracts such as the Lomé Sugar Agreement and by abolishing all trade restrictions, especially in the fields where the lldcs could develop a comparative advantage. In the field of industrialisation and technology, development cannot be left to the market forces alone. A positive and subsidised industrialisation policy and technology transfer would be required to overcome the lldc's structurally disadvantaged position, along the lines adopted by most developed countries to stimulate their own deprived regions. More generally, a certain degree of delinking with the rest of the world economy could be favoured since there is a tendency to extract surplus from these countries in terms of both human and investment capital. In the field of aid, it would mean first that aid should not only be geared to meet basic needs, but also to foster this structural transformation by encouraging, for example, industrialisation based on the lldcs' existing resource base. Second, there is a strong case for a legal right for external assistance and for an automatic transfer mechanism. This would lessen many of the disadvantages of tied aid. The features of such a framework could combine aspects of the legally oriented Lomé Convention, the IMF macro-economic budget approach, and the bilateral aid approach. One desirable side effect would be that a much larger part of aid would be given as untied programme aid instead of project aid. Such an automatic transfer mechanism should not obviate the obligation of receiving countries to be accountable for their economic and social policies. But this would be done on a *legal and objective basis.* All donor and receiving countries could participate in such a legal framework.

Being the most important aid and trade partners of the lldcs, and therefore the most important external influence in these countries, the European states and EEC institutions are in a strong position to promote a structural transformation of these economies instead of continuing a policy primarily based on shortsighted political motives.

Notes

1 The 31st lldc, Guinea-Bissau, joined the list only on 1 September 1981; this is why the tables in this Chapter list only 30 states.
2 OECD *Development Co-operation 1978*, p. 25 (Paris 1978).
3 Guinea-Bissau, Guinea, Cape Verde, Benin, Chad, Ethiopia, Mali, Tanzania, Somalia, Yemen P.D.R., Afghanistan, Laos. A number of other countries have quite unstable governments in this respect: Uganda, Yemen A.R., C.A.R.

9
EEC Policies towards the least developed: an Analysis

Adrian Hewitt

The EEC, and particularly its policy proposing body, the Commission, was an active participant in the formulation of the Substantial New Action Programme (SNAP) for the least developed countries, prepared for the September UN Conference on the least developed countries (lldcs). On account of the concentration of lldcs (by number, though less so in terms of population) in the African continent – in particular in the Sahel region[1] – and hence within the ACP group, the EEC can legitimately claim that much of its development policy is oriented towards the needs of the least developed. This appears true not only in terms of country aid allocations – 64 % of Lomé I aid allocations were directed towards the least developed ACP states, a figure boosted to 70 % under Lomé II aid programming – but also in terms of its proposed sectoral shift in project aid allocations – less to infrastructure, more towards agricultural development and in particular expansion of domestic food production capacity, and towards the promotion of domestic energy sources. Moreover, in terms of trade access, almost no tariff restrictions remain for any ACP exporters of manufactures (not that the lldcs have any significant export capacity here), while lldcs worldwide are offered duty-free access to the Community market for a specifically designed range of agricultural items (including processed products) under the EEC's Generalised System of Preferences (see Chapter 5). No fewer than twenty separate clauses of the legally-binding second Lomé Convention deal with special provisions for the least developed ACP states. They crop up in each of the functional sections (titles) of the convention with the sole exception of the section on investment guarantees. As regards food aid, the largest lldc, Bangladesh, is currently the leading recipient of EEC food aid. Finally, as regards tariff preferences for non-ACP states, the EEC's new GSP scheme declares one of its aims to be the provision of practical assistance (through trade access measures) to the least developed countries in particular.

This chapter examines the special measures for lldcs outlined in the EEC's policy documents for application in the 1980s, identifying those which are likely to be of practical value. It then surveys the results of EEC assistance in its various forms to the least developed countries in the past, and concludes with a closer scrutiny of the lldc category as applied by the Community.

Special measures under Lomé II.

Several of the countries classified in Lomé II as 'least developed' do not appear on the UN list of lldcs – examples are Togo, Mauritania, Sierra Leone and Swaziland. The confusion arising from this difference in categorisation is important since EEC-recognised lldcs have been applying for UN status as lldcs on the basis of EEC selection policy, much to the distaste of some other members of the Group of 77. Moreover, some of the preferences granted under Lomé to lldcs apply also to islands and landlocked states, not all of which qualify as least developed. Those ACP

Table 9.1 *Classification of the poorest countries*

	UN (lldc)	*Lomé Convention (lldc)*	*World Bank (Low income)*	*UN (MSA)*	*Number of mentions*
Benin	*	*	*	*	4
Burundi	*	*	*	*	4
Botswana	*	*			2
Cape Verde	*	*	*	*	4
C.A.R.	*	*	*	*	4
Chad	*	*	*	*	4
Comoros	*	*	*		3
Ethiopia	*	*	*	*	4
Gambia	*	*	*	*	4
Guinea	*	*	*	*	4
Guinea Bisssau	*	*	*	*	4
Malawi	*	*	*		3
Mali	*	*	*	*	4
Lesotho	*	*	*	*	4
Niger	*	*	*	*	4
Rwanda	*	*	*	*	4
Somalia	*	*	*	*	4
Sudan	*	*	*	*	4
Tanzania	*	*	*	*	4
Uganda	*	*	*	*	4
Upper Volta	*	*	*	*	4
Afghanistan	*		*	*	3
Bangladesh	*		*	*	3

Table 9.1 (*continued*)

	UN (lldc)	*Lomé Convention (lldc)*	*World Bank (Low income)*	*UN (MSA)*	*Number of mentions*
Bhutan	*		*		2
Laos	*		*	*	3
Maldive Is.	*		*		2
Nepal	*		*	*	3
Yemen (AR)	*			*	2
Yemen (PDR)	*			*	2
W. Samoa	*	*		*	3
Haiti	*		*	*	3
Djibouti		*			1
Dominica		*			1
Grenada		*			1
Mauritania		*		*	2
Sao Tome y Principe		*			1
Seychelles		*			1
Sierra Leone		*	*	*	3
Soloman Is.		*			1
St. Lucia		*			1
Swaziland		*			1
Togo		*	*		2
Tonga		*			1
Tuvalu		*			1
Burma			*	*	2
China (PR)			*		1
India			*	*	2
Indonesia			*		1
Kampuchea			*	*	2
Madagascar			*	*	2
Mozambique			*	*	2
Pakistan			*	*	2
Sri Lanka			*	*	2
Vietnam			*		1
Zaire			*		1
Cameroon				*	1
Egypt				*	1
El Salvador				*	1
Ghana				*	1
Guatemala				*	1
Guyana				*	1
Honduras				*	1
Ivory Coast				*	1
Kenya				*	1
Senegal				*	1
Total per list	31	35	41	45	—

states which for Lomé II purposes are 'least developed' regardless of their geographical situation number thirty-five, ie more than half of the ACP (see Table 9.1). The special measures designed specifically for them in the Convention fall into seven separate categories:

- *Trade cooperation*: Articles 15 and 21
- *Stabex*: Article 46
- *Minerals*: Article 53
- *Industrial Cooperation*: Article 82
- *Agricultural Cooperation*: Article 90
- *Financial and technical cooperation* (aid): Articles 106, 107, 112, 125, 129, 135, 139, 141, 145, 152, and 153
- *Protocol No. 1* (on rules of origin requirements): Article 30

The profusion of special mentions for lldcs under the aid section of the convention demonstrates that this is the instrument by which the EEC – and indeed the North – feels it can best stimulate development in the lldcs. However, it is of the nature of legal documents that frequency of mention does not necessarily imply substantive significance. A closer analysis of the special provisions for lldcs built into the legal framework of the treaty shows that most of the articles mentioning the lldcs merely embody a general statement of intentions to take into account their special needs.[2] By far the most important of the specific lldc provisions are the special terms offered for the EEC's two main financing mechanisms – Stabex and project aid. These are analysed below. In addition the Box lists other special provisions that offer small but tangible benefits to the ACP least developed.

Article 46: Stabex

ACP lldcs benefit from lower dependence and trigger thresholds (both set at 2 % instead of 6.5 % under Lomé II), as do the island and landlocked states. The lower dependence threshold enlarges the range of products covered by the scheme for many lldcs; the lower trigger threshold merely signifies that the EEC Commission is prepared to process small claims, so long as they come from the least developed countries. More important is that the lldcs do not have to repay Stabex transfers under any circumstances. This is a very valuable concession to the least developed, particularly as Stabex is easily the fastest disbursing component of the Lomé aid programme. A further sub-group of the least developed – a dozen countries which theoretically trade more with third parties than with the EEC – are given Stabex cover for their non-EEC exports too. Finally, in the event of adequate Stabex funds being unavailable to satisfy the ACP's legitimate demands, the lldcs are to be treated less unfavourably than the other ACP countries. As explained in Chapter 1, this provision came into force in 1981 and is likely to do so again.

Minor concessions to the least developed under Lomé II

Article 21: guarantees that ACP lldcs will not have to cover their own costs when participating in trade fairs: expenses incurred in shipping goods and for official attendance are financed by the EEC. The value of such a provision, though obviously small overall, depends substantially on the use made of it by the ACP governments, but it removes one disincentive from export promotion.

Article 112: promises to take into account the special problems of lldcs when appraising aid projects. Implicit in this measure is the acceptance of a lower rate of return than would otherwise be acceptable. This gives the EEC more latitude in enlarging the absorptive capacity for lldcs, though it would be counter-productive if the measure were to permit unviable and unsustainable investments to be financed simply because the lldcs in question had omitted to identify any more acceptable projects.

Article 129: promises short-cut measures with regard to aid implementation and the award of contracts. With the proviso that minimum criteria still have to be met, this ought to be a beneficial measure for lldcs from the point of view of rapidity of disbursement.

Article 30 of Protocol No. 1: promises, somewhat curiously, that requests for derogations from the rules of origin should, when emanating from an lldc, be treated (by the EEC) with 'a favourable bias', particularly in respect of the employment effects and in respect of the duration of the derogation. While the uncertainty this clause affords is hardly conducive to encouraging investment in lldc processing or manufacturing for export, it is arguable that it could provide some welcome surprises to ACP lldc exporters of processed foods and (if any) of manufactures.

Article 106: Project aid allocation and financial terms

Special treatment is given to lldcs in determining the overall volume of their indicative aid programme. The special attention accorded to lldcs in dividing up the EDF 'aid cake' at the beginning of each five year period overrides the Commission's normal criteria for aid allocation between ACP countries, which is otherwise based primarily on population size, adjusted to take into account per capita income, geographical position, bilateral aid receipts from EEC donors, and some political considerations as perceived by the Commission.[3] The application of these criteria is far from rigorous, but the pride of place given to the lldc group criterion is important. Hence lldcs occupied 11 of the top 15 positions in the Lomé I aid allocations (only the relatively populous countries Zaire, Kenya, Madagascar and Senegal were interspersed in the top bracket) though a very different pattern emerges when aid *disbursements* are considered (see Table 9.2).

Table 9.2 *Comparison of Lomé I indicative programmes and actual receipts of aid, as at 31 December 1979, by ACP state, ranked in order of volume*

	(1) Lomé I Indicative Programme Allocation		*(2) Of which disbursed at 31 Dec 1979*		*(3) Total EDF IV disbursements (including Stabex) at 31 Dec 1979*	
	Amount (mEUA)	*Rank*	*Amount* (mEUA)	*Rank*	*Amount* (mEUA)	*Rank*
Ethiopia[a]	117.8	1	14.6	19	29.0	9
Tanzania[a]	103.4	2	23.9	10	44.6	4
Zaire	96.5	3	27.4	5	27.4	12
Sudan[a]	90.6	4	15.3	17	17.9	19
Uganda[a]	73.6	5	2.4	43	16.1	24
Mali[a]	73.0	6	30.5	2	36.4	5
Kenya	72.0	7	28.8	4	28.8	10 =
Madagascar	69.2	8	13.5	20	16.4	22
Niger[a]	68.5	9	42.9	1	65.6	2
Upper Volta[a]	68.0	10	26.9	6	34.1	6
Malawi[a]	67.2	11	21.6	12	21.6	18
Guinea[a]	64.0	12	12.8	22	12.8	27
Somalia[a]	63.6	13	13.3	21	15.2	25
Senegal	59.0	14	26.1	7	91.2	1
Rwanda[a]	58.7	15	29.0	3	29.6	8
Burundi[a]	58.1	16	15.5	16	17.0	21
Cameroon	55.3	17	24.7	9	28.8	10 =
Chad[a]	51.9	18	25.2	8	25.2	12
Ghana	48.0	19	11.1	23	16.3	23
Zambia	45.1	20	22.8	11	22.8	17
Benin	44.3	21	8.5	25	23.9	15
Ivory Coast	40.0	22	14.9	18	29.9	7
Central African Republic[a]	37.3	23	9.5	24	10.4	29
Togo	35.7	24	20.0	13	23.6	16
Mauritania	33.6	25	16.2	15	53.2	3
Sierra Leone	31.1	26	4.9	32 =	8.9	31
Congo	25.0	27 =	17.2	14	24.6	14
Liberia	25.0	27 =	6.2	29	13.8	26
Lesotho[a]	22.0	29	5.6	31	5.6	35
Guinea Bissau[a]	20.0	30 =	8.4	26	17.2	20
Jamaica	20.0	30.0 =	5.9	30	5.9	34
Botswana[a]	19.0	32	6.7	27	6.7	32 =
Suriname	18.0	33	1.3	48	1.3	51
Mauritius	15.3	34	4.9	32 =	4.9	37
Guyana	12.8	35	2.7	40 =	2.7	44
Swaziland	12.0	36	6.4	28	9.8	30
Gambia[a]	11.3	37	2.7	40 =	5.2	36
Solomon Islands	10.7	38	0.1	56	2.3	47 =
Trinidad and Tobago	10.3	39	3.1	39	3.1	43
Papua New Guinea	10.0	40	3.3	38	3.3	42
Fiji	9.9	41	4.6	34	6.7	32 =
Gabon	9.0	42	4.3	35	11.0	28

Table 9.2 (*continued*)

	(1) Lomé I Indicative Programme Allocation		*(2) Of which disbursed at 31 Dec 1979*		*(3) Total EDF IV disbursements (including Stabex) at 31 Dec 1979*	
	Amount (mEUA)	*Rank*	*Amount* (mEUA)	*Rank*	*Amount* (mEUA)	*Rank*
Equatorial Guinea	7.0	43	0.3	54	0.3	56
Comoros[a]	6.3	44	2.6	42	4.5	38
W Samoa[a]	4.6	45	1.4	46=	4.2	39
Cape Verde[a]	4.0	46	1.7	45	2.5	45=
Djibouti	3.9	47	1.2	49	1.9	50
Kiribati	3.5	48	—	57=	2.3	47=
Saint Lucia	3.2	49	0.5	51=	0.5	53=
Tonga	3.2	50	1.4	46=	2.5	45=
Barbados	2.6	51	2.0	44=	2.0	49
Dominica	2.5	52	4.1	36	4.1	40
Seychelles	2.4	53	0.7	50	0.7	52
Grenada	2.0	54	0.2	55	0.2	57=
Bahamas	1.8	55	0.4	53	0.4	55
Sao Tome and Principe	1.8	56	0.5	51=	0.5	53=
Nigeria	0.9	57	4.0	37	4.0	41
Tuvalu	0.6	58	—	57=	0.2	57=
Saint Vincent	—	59	—	57=	—	59
Total (59 ACP states)	1,929.4		606.7		901.6	

Notes: Column (3) does not include disbursements of 85.6 mEUA for the benefit of more than one ACP country. Disbursements include expenditure on EEC Delegations in ACP countries.

[a] Countries on the UN lldc list.

Source: House of Lords Select Committee on the European Communities: *Report on Development Aid Policy*, 1981.

The priority accorded to lldcs in allocating indicative programme volumes from the programmable part of the EDF is reinforced by the financial terms offered to lldcs. Many lldcs are given project aid solely in the form of grants. Those which receive more than 15 mn ecu of aid (over the five year programme) are allocated some in soft loan form, but overall the lldcs will receive not less than 80 % of their Lomé II aid in grants. For non-lldcs ACPs, the share of EDF loans can be as much as 30 %. Moreover, lldcs are given more favourable financial terms even on their soft loans: the rate of interest is fixed at 0.75 % (instead of 1 %) and they are accorded a ten year grace period before commencing amortisation payments.

Other lldc provisions of practical importance are:
Article 135: Gives priority to lldc claims for regional project aid including projects involving neighbouring non-ACP ldcs. This is a valuable provision since the regional component (10 % of the EDF) is the only part of the fund from which an ACP can engineer an increase in its EEC project aid above the level fixed in its indicative programme.
Article 125: allows possible derogations from the strict rules on third country procurement for EEC-financed aid projects. This measure is designed to eliminate excessive cost burdens on the lldc, both for current project financing and for subsequent maintenance of equipment. Derogations still however have to be approved on a case by case basis, as is the case for non-lldcs.
Article 53: fixes lower thresholds for product coverage under the Minex scheme. Lldcs have to show a 10 % export earnings dependence on a listed mineral, instead of the normal 15 %. The impact of this provision is however limited to a couple of lldcs: only Togo (for phosphates), Guinea (for bauxite) currently qualify even given the 10 % threshold. Rwanda's tin exports no longer reach 10 %, and Mauritania (for iron ore) is not yet covered by Minex under the terms of the Convention (iron ore is covered, anomalously, by Stabex until 1984[4]).

Clearly, the enhanced volume of the indicative aid programme for lldcs within Lomé, and the removal of the obligation to repay Stabex are the most important concessions in practical terms. Table 9.2 shows that Niger, Mauritania, Tanzania, Mali and Upper Volta (all lldcs under Lomé definitions, all except Mauritania lldcs under UN rules) were the leading recipients of EDF *disbursements*, after Senegal. Moreover, in June 1981, when the EEC decided that its Stabex fund was inadequate to meet the requests of ACP countries, it negotiated a differential scale of reductions to Stabex transfers, cutting the lldcs by 40 % while reducing transfers to other ACP by 53 %.

The non-Lomé lldcs.

What of the Asian lldcs, and Haiti, which do not fall in the relatively privileged ACP group? The EEC now runs a small but expanding aid programme to what it terms the 'non-associates', a group which includes Latin America as well as the whole of developing Asia, plus Mozambique and Angola. A programme to such a wide range of countries and limited size (see Table 9.3) clearly can make little impact on the lldcs among the 'non-associates'. But Bangladesh has been one of the main recipients of the EEC's 'non-associates' aid, as it has of EEC food aid deliveries: in 1979 it was allocated 100,000 tons of wheat and 3,000 tons of butteroil.

The least developed countries (UN list) are as a whole offered special tariff preferences over other non ACP ldcs and over industrial country exporters to facilitate access to the EEC market under the GSP scheme.

Table 9.3 *Summary of net Community aid disbursements, 1979, by major category*

		mEUA	*Per cent (excluding 2A)*	*Per cent (including 2A)*
1. Aid to ACP countries (Lomé Convention)		420	53	39
2. Food aid (worldwide) at world market prices	259	259	33	—
2A. CAP export refunds on food aid.	301			
	560		—	51
3. Aid to Maghreb and Mashreq countries, Turkey, Cyprus and Malta[a]		45[a]	6[a]	4[a]
4. Emergency aid (worldwide)		30	4	3
5. Aid to non-associates[b]		33[b]	4[b]	3[b]
Total		787	100	100
Total including 2A	1,088			

[a] Includes disbursements in 1978 and 1979.
[b] Includes disbursements in all years since 1976.

Source: House of Lords Select Committee on the European Communities: *Report on Development Aid Policy*, 1981.

Since the ACP have relatively unrestricted and duty-free trade access under the terms of Lomé, this concession is relevant for the nine residual non ACP lldcs – Afghanistan, Bangladesh, Bhutan, Haiti, Laos, the Maldives, Nepal and the two Yemens. Provided each state's exporters can meet the rules of origin requirements, they can export all manufactures duty-free and without facing tariff quotas under the 1981 GSP scheme. The same applies to GSP-covered agricultural products, with the exception of tobacco and instant coffee. Special measures have been taken by the EEC to add two agricultural products for the benefit of particular lldcs, which would not otherwise be included in GSP: raisins (where Afghanistan receives a significant margin of preference over the traditional USA and Australian suppliers) and coffee beans (where Haiti is given a preference over Brazil, Colombia etc., and is put onto the same competitive basis as the ACP coffee producers). Other details of the GSP scheme can be found in Chapter 5. In terms of practical effects, however, it must be noted that no lldc can yet meet the EEC's rules of origin requirements for manufactures exports. Since lldcs as such are not permitted to count cumulative processing in other developing countries as proof of ldc origin (contrary to the ACP group and even the ASEAN group) one solution would be for the lldcs to form a group themselves and gain recognition by the EEC for rules of origin purposes. The tariff concessions on agricultural products have not generally been significant, though if tobacco had been included in the scheme, this would have been of value to Bangladesh. Overall, the non-ACP lldcs as yet get few practical benefits from the EEC's development policy.

The lldc classification issue.

The lldcs were first identified and recognised by the UN General Assembly in December 1971. Key criteria for this new grouping then were:

- per capita GNP below $100 in 1968,
- adult literacy rate below 20%,
- industrial production below 10% of GDP.

None of the original 25 countries identified in 1971 has since been removed from the list, but the total of officially recognised UN lldcs now runs to 31 (see Table 9.1), Guinea Bissau being the latest addition approved shortly before the 1981 Paris Conference. However, in addition to the UN list, there are other lists of ldcs identified by different bodies as being especially needy. There are confusing (and often politically motivated) discrepancies between the memberships of the different lists and their usage.

The EEC uses the UN lldc list for the application of the special measures under its GSP. This is because these special measures were introduced after the 1971 UN decision, and the GSP itself became operational only from 1971 onwards. Moreover, the scheme is administered by the globally-oriented external affairs Directorate General (DG1) of the Commission.

The specially conceived Lomé Convention list of lldcs however, includes all the UN lldcs in Africa, and more besides, while naturally excluding the Asian lldcs and Haiti (which has had its application to join the Lomé Convention rejected). Scrutiny of Table 9.1 shows that only a couple of the exclusively Lomé lldcs appear in the World Bank's low income category (although the bulk of the Asian UN lldcs do, including the most populous). However, neither the UN nor the Lomé list include India, Pakistan or Sri Lanka, which are least developed in terms of per capita income but not in terms of the additional social and sectoral criteria used in the UN classification. If low per capita income is considered as the chief determinant of aid need, as it is for access to the World Bank's IDA soft credits, their exclusion appears as an unhelpful omission.

One further approach would be to concentrate resources on the 'most seriously affected' (MSA) developing countries, those identified by the UN as most vulnerable to the consequences of the 1973 oil shock. Most of the neediest African and Asian countries do appear in this list, but the list is now showing some obsolescence, and hence may be ceasing to have practical applications: for instance, listed countries such as Cameroon and Egypt are now near to self-sufficiency in oil, while others, including the Ivory Coast, have good future prospects. As the table shows, moreover, a category which encompasses nearly half the members of the Group of 77 (itself some 120 countries in all) ends up by being over-comprehensive for the needs of policy-makers, who perhaps inevitably wish to concentrate resources for assistance on a narrower range of countries, where the selection is invariably dictated by complex factors arising out of the balance of national or corporate policy. For instance, the UK uses yet another list of 'poorest countries' for bilateral aid purposes. (See Table 9.4).

Table 9.4 *List of 'Poorest Countries' as currently used by ODA*

	GNP per capita in 1978 **($)**		*GNP per capita in 1978* **($)**
Bangladesh[a]	90	Benin[a]	230
Laos[a]	90	Gambia[a]	230
Bhutan[a]	100	Tanzania[a]	230
Ethiopia[a]	120	Pakistan	230
Mali[a]	120	Afghanistan[a]	240
Nepal[a]	120	Republic of Central Africa[a]	250
Somalia[a]	120	Madagascar	250
Burundi[a]	130	Haiti[a]	260
Chad[a]	140	Mauritania	270
Mozambique	140	Lesotho[a]	280
Burma	150	Angola	300
Maldive Republic[a]	150	Kenya	320
Cape Verde Islands[a]	160	Sudan[a]	320
Upper Volta[a]	160	Togo	320
Vietnam	170	Kampuchea	na
Comoro Islands[a]	180	Uganda[a]	na
India	180	Yemen (PDR)[a]	420
Malawi[a]	180	Yemen Arab Republic[a]	580
Rwanda[a]	180	Botswana[a]	620
Sri Lanka	190	Western Samoa[a]	na
Guinea Bissau	200		
Guinea[a]	210		
Sierra Leone	210		
Zaire	210		
Niger[a]	220		

[a] On the UN list of Least Developed Countries.

Source: Overseas Development Administration.

It could be argued that the lack of congruence between the EEC (Lomé) and UN lists of lldcs is probably not harmful. But it remains paradoxical that the regionally-oriented Directorate-General for Development (DG8) of the Commission should use a different list for Lomé purposes from that used by DGI for trade relations, all the more so because the Lomé relationship itself dates from a time (1975) after the establishment of the UN lldc list. It suggests that the roots of Lomé are still firmly anchored in the EEC's aid philosophy of the 1960s.

Notes

1 See ODI Briefing Paper: 'The Sahel: Problems and Prospects' London, 1981.

2 The purely rhetorical clauses are in articles 15, 82, 90, 107, 141, 145, 152, and 153, which are general statements or promise special attention which has not materialised, or represent 'double counting', since the preferences they promise are already dealt with in other, more substantial clauses. Article 15 appears superficially to be important since it promises special attention for lldcs in the event of the EEC imposing trade safeguards. However trade access for the ACP has never been withdrawn by direct means. Subtler protectionist measures such as 'voluntary export restraints' or health sanctions are used, and could equally well be directed at any competitive lldc exporter.

3 The member states theoretically play no part in the allocation of EDF aid to individual countries. See the statement by the UK Minister for Overseas Development in the White Paper on Development Aid Policy, July 1981 Cmnd 8236.

4 Renegotiation of the Lomé Convention will begin before the full transfer to Minex can be applied.

Statistical Appendix

Table 1 *Source of EEC (9 members) imports by value and by main trading bloc, 1975–80* (Ecu mn)

	1975	*1976*	*1977*	*1978*	*1979*	*1980*	*1980 value as % of world total*
Imports from:							
Class I[a]	60 326	75 818	82 357	92 750	111 365	134 114	49
Class II[b]	54 976	70 021	75 278	71 192	88 282	114 562	42
of which ACP[c]	8 716	10 480	12 502	11 892	14 835	18 924	7
Class III[d]	9 237	12 362	13 326	14 008	17 753	21 943	8
Miscellaneous	911	1 388	782	436	721	947	–

[a] Western industrialised countries, excluding intra-EEC trade.
[b] Developing countries, excluding Cuba 1976–1980.
[c] 54 states, 1975–79, 59 states 1980.
[d] State trading countries – including Cuba 1976–80; excluding West German trade with East Germany.

Source: Eurostat.

Table 2 *Direction of EEC (9 members) exports by value and by main trading bloc, 1975–80* (Ecu mn)

	1975	*1976*	*1977*	*1978*	*1979*	*1980*	*1980 value as % of world total*
Exports to:							
Class I[a]	62 505	74 131	85 643	89 983	104 904	118 978	53
Class II[b]	44 068	50 951	61 875	66 523	69 687	83 388	37
of which ACP[c]	8 124	9 888	12 519	12 723	11 816	15 684	7
Class III[d]	13 014	14 238	14 540	15 436	17 264	18 721	8
Miscellaneous	1 625	1 980	2 230	1 951	2 309	3 358	2

[a] Western industrialised countries, excluding intra-EEC trade.
[b] Developing countries, excluding Cuba 1976–80.
[c] 54 states, 1975–79, 59 states 1980.
[d] State trading countries – including Cuba 1976–80; excluding West German trade with East Germany.

Source: Eurostat.

Table 3 *EEC trade balances with principal Third World trade partners 1975–79* (Ecu mn)[a]

Country	*1975*	*1976*	*1977*	*1978*	*1979*
Morocco	239	477	699	498	661
Algeria	776	607	1578	1632	1052
Tunisia	355	425	418	552	436
Libya	−659	−1897	−1280	−652	−1489
Egypt	1033	842	979	875	1138
Sudan	130	189	266	271	232
Senegal	13	31	47	155	179
Liberia	347	322	426	−54	−45
Ivory Coast	−209	−355	624	−378	−310
Ghana	−5	5	−52	−9	−50
Nigeria	−436	91	1125	1307	1785
Cameroon	−12	−37	−99	−99	−2
Gabon	−47	70	22	−172	−265
Zaire	−219	−504	−637	−714	−673
Kenya	96	40	−74	220	143
Zambia	−128	−152	−219	−100	−291
Panama	247	267	111	162	113
Cuba	363	241	236	118	85
Netherlands Antilles	−93	−65	149	200	60
Colombia	−105	−256	−280	−378	−324
Venezuela	326	557	1596	1292	438
Peru	246	50	−12	−6	59
Brazil	95	−538	−1231	−930	−1229
Chile	−276	−468	−348	−375	−573
Argentina	−74	−621	−798	−882	−383
Syria	119	381	254	291	441
Pakistan	202	244	394	348	430
India	173	−281	−256	244	176
Thailand	11	−234	−220	−331	−249
Indonesia	349	444	227	92	−291
Malaysia	−276	−675	−781	−581	360
Singapore	311	267	283	418	−111
Philippines	−21	−48	−110	−32	777
South Korea	−145	−482	−606	−423	−5161
Taiwan	−272	−396	−593	−542	−1032
Hong Kong	−655	−1014	−842	−584	na

[a] Nine member states; positive number means EEC has an export surplus.

Source: Eurostat.

Table 4 *Commodity composition of EEC imports from Third World 1975–79*[a] (Ecu mn)

	1975	*1976*	*1977*	*1978*	*1979*	*1979 value as % of total*
Commodity group:[b]						
0+1	1 130	1 318	1 225	1 324	1 413	8
2+4	1 484	1 969	1 999	1 816	2 063	12
3	2 800	4 147	4 296	4 648	6 789	38
5	519	680	969	998	1 342	8
6+8	2 523	3 298	3 634	3 766	4 671	26
7	751	797	908	1 031	1 660	6

[a] Nine EEC member states; Third World excludes Cuba 1976–79.
[b] Commodity groups: 0 + 1 – food, beverages and tobacco.
2 + 4 – raw materials.
3 – mineral fuels, lubricants and related materials.
5 – chemicals and related products.
6 + 8 – manufactured goods.
7 – machinery and transport equipment.

Source: Eurostat.

Table 5 *EEC Trade with the Maghreb, 1972–80*[a] (Ecu million)

	Tunisia		*Morocco*		*Algeria*	
	Imports	*Exports*	*Imports*	*Exports*	*Imports*	*Exports*
1972	272.7	192.0	364.9	430.7	942.3	763.8
1973	341.8	191.2	498.9	581.7	1 233.4	1 069.1
1974	548.8	423.6	787.4	910.9	2 054.9	2 128.5
1975	709.8	357.3	1 045.1	805.9	2 819.8	2 049.8
1976	834.7	408.6	1 310.3	779.5	2 747.3	2 152.3
1977	977.1	552.2	1 524.3	834.3	3 674.2	2 095.9
1978	1 120.5	565.2	1 341.9	840.8	3 635.1	2 001.4
1979	1 232.5	790.3	1 676.8	1 012.4	3 999.6	2 422.2
1980	1 541.3	1 098.0	1 479	1 169	4 710	4 027

[a] Total for Nine member states.

Source: EEC Commission.

Table 6 *EEC Trade with the Mashreq 1972–80*[a] (Ecu million)

	Egypt		*Lebanon*		*Syria*		*Jordan*	
	Imports	*Exports*	*Imports*	*Exports*	*Imports*	*Exports*	*Imports*	*Exports*
1972	278.5	136.4	383.7	76.2	151.4	77.8	66.6	2.5
1973	396.3	186.2	476.2	83.2	213.6	105.8	77.4	1.8
1974	812.9	263.5	779.6	200.4	476.7	245.6	138.8	2.6
1975	1349.7	318.4	613.1	82.5	583.9	464.1	218.6	8.2
1976	1475.4	675.2	145.8	40.1	1027.2	649.2	454.2	13.1
1977	1679.8	700.6	601.2	31.9	858.6	601.5	371.0	9.6
1978	1820.9	943.1	607.6	27.6	799.5	504.9	387.2	15.2
1979	2324.0	1182.1	818.4	38.0	1053.0	611.2	531.0	18.0
1980	3105	1746	1032	44	1245	930	687	23

[a] Total for Nine member states.

Source: EEC Commission

Table 7 *Commitments of financial assistance under the Lomé Convention up to end 1980 by method of financing and administering organisation* (in Ecu million)

	Administered by					
	the Commission		*EIB*		*Total*	
	Value	%	*Value*	%	*Value*	%
EDF IV Resources						
– Grants	1 743.3	69	65.0	12	1 808.3	59
of which:						
Interest rate subsidies	–	–	65.0	12	65.0	2
Exceptional aid	146.0	6	–	–	146.0	5
– Special loans	393.8	16	–	–	393.8	13
– Risk capital	–	–	99.0	18	99.0	3
– Stabex	374.0	15	–	–	374.0	12
EIB Resources						
– Loans	–		390.0	70	390.0	13
Total	2 511.1	100	554.0	100	3 065.1	100

Source: EEC Commission

Table 8 *Sectoral distribution of commitments from EDF IV to ACP up to 31 December 1980*

Sector	*Amount Ecu million*	%
Development of Production	1 386.1	45
Industrial development	862.6	
Tourism	16.8	
Rural production	506.7	
Transport and Telecommunications infrastructure	584.3	19
Social Development	380.8	12
Education and training	227.8	
Health	47.4	
Water engineering, housing and urban administration	105.6	
Trade Promotion	32.6	1
Exceptional Aid	146.0	5
Stabex	374.0	12
Miscellaneous (including Delegations)	146.1	5

Source: EEC Commission.

Table 9 *Stabex transfers to ACP and OCT, 1975–80, by country*

Recipient	*1980* *Eua '000*	*1975–1980* *Eua '000*	%
Belize	–	342.4	–
Benin	–	20 366.7	4
Burundi	11 023.6	12 509.3	2
Cameroon	–	4 065.0	1
Cape Verde	214.8	1 421.4	–
C.A.R.	968.4	8 798.0	2
Chad	2 539.9	9 876.1	2
Comoros	1 098.9	3 425.3	1
Congo	–	7 361.7	1
Djibouti	–	691.9	–
Dominica	2 527.9	5 420.8	1
Ethiopia	–	14 420.1	3
Fiji	842.3	2 957.3	1
Gabon	–	6 703.3	1
Gambia	8 117.4	15 632.2	3
Ghana	–	5 176.4	1
Guinea Bissau	1 533.7	12 822.0	2
Ivory Coast	19 195.4	34 195.4	6
Jamaica	3 239.0	3 239.0	1
Kenya	10 032.2	10 032.2	2
Kiribati	497.7	2 781.1	1
Lesotho	242.3	242.3	–
Liberia	–	7 586.9	1
Madagascar	1 211.2	6 958.7	1
Malawi	1 331.0	1 331.0	–
Mali	2 551.6	12 332.5	2
Mauritania	–	37 000.5	7
New Hebrides	–	1 430.9	–
Niger	–	22 654.0	4
Rwanda	6 555.0	7 163.8	1
St. Lucia	1 349.5	1 349.5	–
St. Vincent	913.3	913.3	–
Senegal	38 607.0	103 713.4	20
Sierra Leone	947.8	4 925.1	1
Solomon Islands	–	2 173.4	–
Somalia	1 839.2	3 771.3	1
Sudan	13 415.6	52 559.1	10
Swaziland	–	13 224.9	3
Tanzania	6 255.0	26 956.6	5
Togo	–	3 626.6	1
Tonga	602.2	1 810.2	
Tuvalu	14.5	189.2	–
Uganda	–	20 595.5	4
Upper Volta	–	7 261.9	1
Vanuatu	4 186.8	4 186.8	1
Western Samoa	1 223.0	4 060.5	1
Total	143 076.0	530 254.7	

Note: Columns may not add up due to rounding.

Source: EEC Commission.

Table 10 *Stabex transfers to ACP and OCT, 1975–80, by commodity*

Commodity	*1980* *Eua '000*	*1975–80* *Eua '000*	*%*
Groundnut products	63 951.4	220 906.3	42
Coffee	54 029.6	68 523.9	13
Iron Ore	–	61 789.5	12
Cotton	2 539.9	45 899.3	9
Rough Timber	–	38 953.1	7
Sisal	–	20 577.4	4
Bananas	9 667.9	15 481.3	3
Copra and Copra Products	1 360.9	9 817.2	2
Tea	1 331.0	9 707.3	2
Raw Hides, Skins & Leather	415.9	9 509.7	2
Palm Nuts and Palm Oil	1 221.7	9 021.8	2
Vanilla	1 211.2	4 114.9	1
Cocoa	1 633.2	2 690.8	1
Cloves	–	2 303.5	–
Sawn Timber	–	1 039.0	–
Essential Oils	852.4	852.4	–
Gum Arabic	–	848.5	–
Coconut Oil	842.3	842.3	–
Pyrethrum	–	608.8	–
Cocoa Paste	–	463.6	–
Mohair	242.3	242.3	–
Ylang-Ylang	–	170.6	–
	139 299.7	526 478.2	

Notes: Columns may not add up due to rounding.
Excludes Eua 3 776.6 to Vanuatu for Copra and Coconut Oil, for which no breakdown between the two products is available.

Source: EEC Commission.

Table 11 *Commitments and Disbursements from EDF IV*
Commitments and disbursements as at 31 December 1980 (in Ecu million)

	Commitments							*Disbursements*
Recipient	*Grants and Special Loans*	*Delegations Expenses*	*Stabex*	*Exceptional Aid*	*EIB Interest Subsidy*	*EIB Risk Capital*	*Total*	*Total*
ACP								
Bahamas	1.8	0.04	0	0	0	0	1.8	0.04
Barbados	2.5	0.8	0	0.05	1.3	0•	4.7	2.8
Benin	30.9	1.8	20.4	0.02	0	0	53.1	36.9
Botswana	18.5	1.0	0	2.7	1.3	1.7	25.2	12.1
Burundi	48.6	1.8	1.5	2.1	0	0.5	54.5	25.3
Cameroon	39.0	3.7	3.6	2.3	4.7	4.6	57.9	38.9
Cape Verde	3.5	0.03	1.2	1.4	0	3.6	9.7	3.8
C.A.R.	36.1	2.3	7.8	1.1	0	0	47.3	21.5
Chad	40.8	2.6	7.3	0.3	0	7.5	58.5	33.3
Comoros	6.3	0.3	0	2.9	0	0.02	9.5	3.6
Congo	25.0	2.2	7.4	0.2	0	3.1	37.9	30.3
Djibouti	2.0	0.02	0	1.3	0	1.0	4.3	1.8
Dominica	0.4	0	0	3.9	0	0	4.3	4.2
Equatorial Guinea	6.7	0.09	0	0.8	0	0	7.1	0.3
Ethiopia	85.4	1.7	14.4	4.8	0	0	106.3	48.0
Fiji	8.9	1.0	0.2	3.5	4.2	0	17.8	10.6
Gabon	8.4	1.6	6.7	0	0	0	16.7	14.0
Gambia	11.3	0.8	7.5	0.7	0	2.4	22.7	11.8
Ghana	44.7	1.9	5.2	2.7	2.4	2.3	59.2	21.8
Grenada	1.9	0.08	0	0.5	0	0	2.5	0.7
Guinea	59.4	1.7	0	3.0	0.5	0.2	64.8	27.5
Guinea Bissau	18.4	1.2	11.3	0.5	0	0	31.4	24.4
Guyana	12.3	1.0	0	0	0	3.2	16.5	4.6

Ivory Coast	35.0	3.5	15 000	0.1	7.2	3.0	63.8	39.8
Jamaica	17.6	1.7	0	1.2	0	0.1	20.6	8.2
Kiribati	0.5	0	0	0	0	0	0.5	0
Kenya	71.1	2.5	0	1.6	9.0	1.2	85.4	39.5
Lesotho	17.6	1.0	0	1.2	0	0.03	19.8	8.3
Liberia	23.4	1.2	7.6	0	1.3	0.3	33.8	17.2
Madagascar	67.1	3.1	4.6	1.7	0	2.3	78.8	27.4
Malawi	61.6	1.5	0	4.0	2.4	1.2	70.7	37.5
Mali	66.3	2.9	9.8	1.0	0	6.1	86.1	64.1
Mauritius	10.5	1.2	0	4.8	2.6	0.04	19.2	7.2
Mauritania	28.0	2.5	37.0	1.7	3.6	0	72.8	55.7
Niger	64.4	3.1	22.7	9.6	1.0	0.9	101.7	71.7
Nigeria	7.4	1.1	0	0	9.6	0	18.1	11.5
Papua New Guinea	3.9	0.6	0	0	1.2	1.9	7.6	3.7
Rwanda	58.7	1.8	0.6	6.4	0	3.0	70.5	44.4
Saint Lucia	0.9	0	0	1.0	0	0	1.9	1.0
St Vincent	0	0	0	0.5	0	0	0.5	0.5
Sao Tomé	1.6	0.1	0	0.3	0	0	2.0	1.2
Senegal	52.5	3.8	65.1	4.6	2.3	8.1	136.4	104.6
Seychelles	2.1	0	0	0	0	0.6	2.7	1.2
Sierra Leone	26.4	1.2	4.0	0	0	0	31.6	13.6
Solomon Islands	6.6	0	0	0	0	0	6.6	0
Somalia	41.2	2.2	1.9	13.4	0	0.2	58.9	33.1
Sudan	90.0	3.0	41.8	4.9	0	6.5	146.2	65.8
Suriname	8.2	1.2	0	0	0	0	9.4	3.6
Swaziland	11.8	0.6	13.2	0.03	1.8	1.1	28.5	21.2
Tanzania	85.0	2.2	20.7	0.4	0.7	7.8	116.8	58.8
Togo	35.1	2.1	3.6	0	2.3	5.2	48.3	29.1
Tonga	2.8	0.2	1.2	0.2	0	0	4.4	3.5
Trinidad & Tobago	5.7	1.3	0	0	1.6	0	8.6	3.7
Tuvalu	0.5	0	0	0	0	0	0.5	0
Uganda	30.4	1.3	20.6	3.5	0	0	55.8	34.6
Upper Volta	56.3	2.8	7.3	0	1.6	8.0	76.0	39.8

Table 11 *(continued)*

	Commitments							Disbursements
Recipient	*Grants and Special Loans*	*Delegations Expenses*	*Stabex*	*Excep-tional Aid*	*EIB Interest Subsidy*	*EIB Risk Capital*	*Total*	*Total*
Western Samoa	4.5	0.3	2.8	0	0	0	7.6	5.5
Zaire	93.4	3.3	0	19.3	0	5.2	121.2	39.2
Zambia	43.6	2.0	0	17.0	1.8	3.4	67.8	34.2
Regional Projects	232.3	0	0	0	0.6	0.1	233.0	98.1
Total	1 876.8	103.4	374.0	146.0	65.0	96.4	2 661.6	1 426.9

Source: EEC Commission.

Table 12 *EIB lending to the ACP, Maghreb and Mashreq in 1980* (in Eua million)

	From EIB own resources		*Special section operations*	
Recipient	*No. of projects*	*Amount*	*No. of projects*	*Amount*
Maghreb	2	25.0	2	20.0
Morocco	0	0	1	5.0
Tunisia	1	5.0	1	15.0
Algeria	1	20.0	0	0
Mashreq	2	7.0	0	0
Jordan	1	4.0	0	0
Lebanon	1	3.0	0	0
Africa	15	95.9	17	20.46
Cape Verde	0	0	1	3.5
Ivory Coast	3	10.0	0	0
Gambia	0	0	1	0.09
Ghana	0	0	1	0.25
Senegal	2	12.0	1	6.4
Kenya	1	7.5	0	0
Swaziland	1	2.0	1	1.0
Guinea	1	4.4	1	0.15
Upper Volta	1	8.0	1	3.5
Nigeria	1	25.0	0	0
Regional West Africa	0	0	1	0.14
Zaire	0	0	1	0.04
Botswana	2	6.5	2	1.75
Comoros	0	0	1	0.01
Malawi	1	5.0	1	0.19
Mauritius	1	7.5	1	0.04
Somalia	0	0	1	0.25
Tanzania	0	0	1	0.35
Zambia	1	8.0	1	2.8
Caribbean	2	10.0	0	0
Barbados	1	5.0	0	0
Trinidad	1	5.0	0	0
Pacific (Fiji)	1	11.5	0	0
	22	134.5	19	40.46

Source: *EIB Annual Report 1979* (Luxembourg).

Table 13 *Breakdown of EDF IV funded contracts according to nationality of suppliers, up to 31 December 1980*

	% share of			
Country of firm	*Works contracts*	*Supply contracts*	*Technical Co-operation contracts*	*All contracts*
Belgium	7.0	4.6	8.7	6.8
Denmark	0.3	0.3	2.5	0.8
France	25.5	21.1	20.3	23.5
Germany	5.6	21.0	19.1	11.6
Ireland	0	0	1.5	0.3
Italy	10.3	18.4	11.1	12.1
Luxembourg	0	0	1.5	0.3
Netherlands	3.9	4.3	7.6	4.8
United Kingdom	3.8	15.1	14.0	8.3
Total EEC	56.4	84.8	86.2	68.5
ACP and TOM	42.3	9.2	13.3	29.4
Third Countries	1.4	6.0	0.5	2.2
Total in Ecu '000	679 606	241 370	239 893	1 160 869

Note: Columns may not add up due to rounding.

Source: EEC Commission.

Table 14 *Allocations to the non-associate aid programme*

	Eua million
1976	20
1977	45
1978	70
1979	110
1980	138.5
1981	150

Source: EEC Commission.

Table 15 *Exchange rates: member states of the EEC and the United States*[a]

Period	*Germany*	*France*	*Italy*	*Netherlands*	*Belgium/ Luxembourg*	*United Kingdom*	*Ireland*	*Denmark*	*United States*
	1 000 DM =. . . Ecu	1 000 FF =. . . Ecu	1 000 Lit =. . . Ecu	1 000 Fl =. . . Ecu	1 000FB/Flux =. . . Ecu	1 000 £ =. . . Ecu	1 000 £ =. . . Ecu	1 000 Dkr =. . . Ecu	1 000 $ =. . . Ecu
1975	327 934	187 997	1 235	318 989	21 945	1 785 631		140 397	805 951
1976	355 183	187 096	1 075	338 392	23 167	1 608 809		147 890	894 414
1977	377 599	178 378	993	357 130	24 460	1 529 751		145 865	876 332
1978	391 252	174 217	925	363 112	24 963	1 506 142		142 462	784 720
1979	398 268	171 543	878	363 816	24 897	1 547 051	1 493 694	138 714	729 581
1980	396 164	170 388	841	362 283	24 632	1 670 880	1 479 297	127 757	718 221

[a] The Ecu is a 'basket' unit, based on a certain quantity of each Community currency, weighted on the basis of the 5 years (1969–1973) average of the gross national product (GNP) and of the intra-Community trade of each member state. This weighting also takes account, for each currency, of the share of the country concerned in the short-term monetary support between the central banks of the Community.

Source: Eurostat.

Documentary Appendix

European Parliament Resolution on Hunger in the World (September 1980)

Joint Declaration by EEC and ACP on the Accession of Greece to the EEC

– Verbal communication from Mr Pisani

Formal Procedure for Approving Non-Associate Aid

Extracts from the Communiqué of the Ottawa Western Economic Summit July 1981

European Parliament Resolution on Hunger in the World (September 1980)

Resolution

on the European Community's contribution to the campaign to eliminate hunger in the world

The European Parliament,

- recalling its resolution of 16 November 1979 on hunger in the world [1],
- having regard to the preparatory work carried out by the Committee on Development and Cooperation, both in its working party and specific reports (Doc. 1-341/80/Ann.) and in the public hearings it has organised,
- having regard to the report of the Committee on Development and Cooperation (Doc. 1-341/80) and opinions of the Political Affairs Committee, the Committee on Agriculture, the Committee on External Economic Relations and the Committee on the Environment, Public Health and Consumer Protection (Doc. 1-341/80/Ann.),
- concerned at the scale of the problem of world hunger and at its consequences for the lives of hundreds of millions of human beings,
- convinced that the chronic undernourishment of the poorest nations is one aspect of the general problem of underdevelopment,
- considering that, in the present international economic and monetary crisis, the imbalance between industrialised and developing countries has increased still further and has become one of the major causes of tension and of the deterioration in the international situation,
- deeply disturbed by the failure of the extraordinary session of the UN General Assembly to reach an agreement on the 'global North-South negotiations'.

1. Affirms that the campaign against hunger must be given priority in the search for fair and lasting solutions to the sources of conflict which are threatening the future of mankind;
2. Appeals to its electorate in an attempt to stimulate the political will needed to overcome the difficulties which are hindering the achievement of this objective;

---

[1] OJ No C 309, 10. 12. 1979, p. 42.

3. Requests the Council and Commission on the basis of the following guidelines and proposals:
(a) to draw up a coherent series of measures for the campaign against hunger with a view to the global North-South negotiations and to the adoption by the UN of a strategy for the Third Development Decade,
(b) to implement, in coordination with the Member States and the various international organisations, a policy which will help to guarantee the developing countries' food supplies;

(a) *with regard to the campaign against hunger in the context of a new relationship between industrialised and underdeveloped countries*
4. Considers that the independent and balanced development of each country or region, taking as its starting point the expansion of the internal market and the production structures of the developing countries and a substantial improvement in the purchasing power of their peoples, is a prerequisite for the elimination of underdevelopment and hunger;
5. Emphasises, in this connection, the need to step up efforts to establish a new more equitable system of international relations; recognises that this implies in particular;
- far-reaching adjustments to the production methods and way of life in the industrialised countries,
- an increasing reallocation of current world expenditure on arms to development aid;
- a massive transfer of financial and technological resources to the least-favoured regions and countries;
6. Notes the proposals contained in the Brandt report and requests the Commission to consider them in detail and to make specific suggestions concerning their possible implementation, in particular with regard to a more universal and automatic system of development finance;
7. Draws attention to the fact that most of the Community Member States have failed to meet the commitment to allocate at least 0.7 % of their gross national product to public development aid; therefore requests the Council to ask the Member States to draw up a timetable giving specific dates for the fulfilment of this commitment as soon as possible;
8. Requests that Community aid as a percentage of Member States' bilateral aid be increased progressively;
9. Is concerned at the growing indebtedness of the developing countries which are simultaneously hit by the crisis in the food and energy sectors and the general economic crisis;
10. Insists that the Community and the Member States contribute to the setting up, as a matter of urgency, of specific measures to relieve the alarming balance of payments problems facing these countries; this in particular involves, in the spirit of the declaration published following the industrialised countries' Summit in Venice:
(a) support for mechanisms for the recycling of petrodollars,
(b) the extension of the World Bank's activities to the financing of programmes aimed at structural adjustments in developing countries,
(c) pressure should be exerted so that all the principal industrialised countries should contribute immediately to the increase, which has already been decided on, of IMF quotas and the reconstitution of IDA resources,

(d) increased use of IMF resources under conditions which would take account of the particular problems of developing countries;

11. Considers the proposals from the WFC and the FAO to be of particular interest, their aim being to enable the developing countries to finance their imports of essential goods, above all food products, by using the facilities provided by the IMF to a greater extent;

12. Considers that, to eliminate mass hunger and undernourishment, it is essential for as many of the developing countries as possible to achieve self-sufficiency in food; for this purpose it is necessary to strengthen the ability of those developing countries which import food products to satisfy their own food requirements by expanding their agricultural development;

13. Requests the Commission and Council to pay particular attention, in all sectors of development policy including the commercial aspects, to the poorest developing countries and those most affected by the problem of hunger;

14. Requests the Commission and Council, in order to help increase the transfer of resources to the rural development of the developing countries, to enter a substantial sum in the 1981 budget for the revival and strengthening of the International Fund for Agricultural Development (IFAD) (in which, on a basis of parity, the industrialised countries, the member countries of OPEC, and the developing countries cooperate on projects aimed at increasing food production and consumption in the poorest developing countries) so that the Community as such can participate in this fund, the resources of which should be increased from 1,000 million to at least 3,000 million dollars;

(b) *with regard to the agricultural and rural development of the developing countries*

15. Takes the view that, in order to satisfy the developing countries' food requirements (which are increasing as a result, *inter alia*, of the rapid population growth) national development programmes must accord high priority to agricultural and rural development;

16. Emphasises that this priority depends in the first instance on a choice to be made by the developing countries but that its implementation depends decisively both on the system of international trade and the economic policies of the more advanced countries and on the technical and financial resources provided by the latter for cooperation in the agricultural and rural sector;

17. Regards with interest the adoption by the developing countries of suitable food strategies at local, national and regional level; considers that the Community should support these strategies and, in particular, calls on the Council and Commission to:

- provide appropriate financial assistance based, *inter alia*, on multiannual financing measures and financing provided jointly with Member States or international organisations;
- guarantee the technical aid needed to enable the developing countries concerned to define and implement their own food strategies;
- include rural development cooperation (above all in connection with the programming of aid) in developing countries' food strategies;
- increase and improve aid for the rural development of the non-associated developing countries but without prejudice to the normal evolution of relations with the ACP countries;

18. Considers that, in the context of the strategies adopted by developing countries, cooperation by the Community in agricultural and rural development should be directed towards a number of vital objectives, in particular:
- to ensure global and balanced growth in which agricultural development and industrial expansion are strictly interdependent;
- to orient production structures more closely to internal requirements without, however, disregarding the importance of exports for the development process;
- to encourage the development of rural areas on the basis of integrated programmes designed to develop agriculture, create craft and agri-industrial activities and improve services and infrastructures, and to do so in a manner which ensures a balanced distribution of the population throughout the country concerned;

19. Stresses the importance for agricultural and rural development of factors such as:
- the adoption of national farm price policies which stimulate production;
- the organisation of a system of agricultural credit adapted to the special situation of small farmers in the developing countries;
- the improvement of production-consumption structures and, in particular, the establishment of marketing networks with a view to the creation of local and regional markets;

20. Considers that, although the necessary measures may vary from one country to another, agrarian reform is an essential prerequisite to rural development and increased production;

21. Emphasises that the rural population and the producers must be directly involved in the development programmes; points out the decisive contribution to the process of participation made by the agricultural workers' associations and by cooperatives; stresses also, in this connection, the role of non-governmental organisations in the implementation of basic rural development projects;

22. Draws attention to the invaluable role played by training and education and calls on the Community to step up cooperation aimed at promoting special programmes in this sector;

23. Acknowledges the vital work carried out by women in the developing countries in the production and distribution of agricultural products and in the preparation of foodstuffs and hopes that this will be taken more fully into account in development programmes and, above all, as regards the social, family, demographic, educational and health aspects of the campaign against hunger;

24. Considers that, to eliminate hunger, it is not only adequate food supplies that are required but also health services and education, drugs to combat diseases connected with undernourishment, etc; therefore calls on the Community to ensure that its technical and financial aid to the developing countries also covers this sector;

25. Stresses that scientific and agronomic research
(a) should be adapted to the special characteristics of the various rural societies and to their development needs,
(b) should contribute both to safeguarding farming traditions and local techniques and to perfecting methods of cultivation and technologies which are suitable for local physical, economic and social conditions and for the energy resources available in each country or region;

26. Requests the Council and Commission to take steps to increase research facilities in the developing countries and to assist its dissemination;

27. Calls for the early opening of the technical centre for agricultural and rural cooperation provided for in the new Convention of Lomé;
28. Considers that the problem of hunger could be reduced by increasing the consumption of fish but that this calls for larger stocks and, in many cases, the encouragement of new eating habits; requests the Council and Commission to devote particular attention to improvements in fishing equipment and techniques and to support the measures taken by the developing countries and by international organisations such as the FAO (particularly its programme for exclusive economic zones) with a view to eliminating the technical and organisational difficulties which in many countries are preventing this resource from being fully exploited;
29. Draws attention to the vast quantities of food which are lost after the harvests and requests the Commission and Council:
(a) in the context of rural development cooperation policy, to provide for practical measures designed to improve harvesting techniques and the arrangements for storage and conservation, particularly with regard to cereals, and
(b) to introduce *ad hoc* training programmes to help ensure that they are implemented on a large scale;
30. Feels that the implementation of the objectives of agricultural and rural development should be accompanied by proper soil management and by a policy designed to preserve or re-establish the ecological balance through the adoption of local, national and regional projects relating in particular to soil consolidation, afforestation, measures to halt the process of desertification and the balanced utilisation of water resources;

(c) *with regard to Community food aid*
31. Considers that Community food aid should be reviewed and adjusted in the light of the security of food supplies and the agricultural and rural development of the developing countries;
32. Requests the Council and Commission to ensure that as far as possible food aid goes hand in hand with practical agricultural and rural development projects, to plan accordingly the technical and financial aid to the ACP countries and the non-associated developing countries and to provide for multiannual food aid commitments;
33. Asks the Council and Commission to allow food aid also to be used to establish emergency reserves in the developing countries;
34. Emphasises the need for Community aid to be adapted more closely to the food requirements of the peoples concerned and recommends more frequent purchases of foodstuffs from the regions and the developing countries which border on the countries receiving the aid ('three-way transactions');
35. Calls on the Commission to strengthen, reorganise and coordinate its services more effectively with a view to:
- improving and speeding up the provision of aid (in particular by means of a basic regulation on transport),
- eliminating abuses and increasing the transparency of aid management, taking account of past criticisms and of those contained in the special report by the Court of Auditors,
- improving and increasing the regularity of controls, beginning with quality control;

36. Requests the Council to adopt the regulation on food aid without further delay;
37. Requests the Commission
(a) to prepare a detailed document on food aid since 1974 and on the prospects for the next few years, and
(b) to submit an annual report on food and emergency aid;
38. Asks that Community aid in cereals be increased beyond the minimum obligation laid down in the new Food Aid Convention as from the 1981 financial year; the 1982 financial commitment should be raised to a level equivalent to a contribution by the Community and the Member States of 2.5 million tonnes (give estimated world requirements of 12.5 million tonnes);
39. Considers, however, that the increase in aid in the form of skimmed-milk powder and butteroil should, under present circumstances, be contingent upon the genuine possibility of direct distribution to the peoples concerned and upon safety guarantees with regard to health; points out, in this connection, that certain Western practices – such as bottle-feeding babies with skimmed-milk powder products – cannot be exported to the developing countries without suitable health education, above all among women;
40. Considering that, in addition to food aid as such, the Community should be in a position to provide effective aid in the event of serious natural or other disasters and considering, also, that experience in recent years has shown that there is a growing need for such aid and that it must be administered with extreme speed and flexibility, feels that it is essential to increase the budget appropriations allocated to emergency aid substantially;
41. Calls on the Council and Commission to make every effort to ensure that the Food Aid Convention is renewed when it expires in July 1981 and that the quantities to be provided are adequately increased;
42. Requests that, at the forthcoming global North-South negotiations, for which agenda the Community has proposed the inclusion of an item 'Food', the Community should make a number of positive offers, in particular:
- additional technical aid for the preparation of food strategies;
- financial and technical aid for the establishment and management of food stocks in the developing countries;
- a voluntary increase in Community aid in cereals to a level higher than the quantities laid down in the new Food Aid Agreement;
- an appropriate contribution to the emergency food reserve and adoption of FAO and WFC proposal to guarantee this reserve by means of an international agreement;

(d) *with regard to international trade in agricultural and food products*
43. Emphasises that, in connection also with the campaign to eliminate mass hunger and undernourishment, the more advanced countries should adapt their commercial policies, above all as regards trade in food and other agricultural products, to the developing countries' requirements relating to greater participation in international trade and the stabilisation of their food supplies;
44. Requests the Commission to carry o a study on:
(a) the effects of the CAP on internatiltrade in foodstuffs
(b) the effects of Community agricultural exports on world markets and on the developing countries;
45. Requests the Commission to raw up a trade policy in the agricultural sector

which would be compatible with the Community's development policy;
46. Calls on the Commission and Council to take immediate action:
(a) gradually to reduce the administrative and tariff barriers which have a detrimental effect on the developing countries' agricultural exports and
(b) as a priority to open up the Community market to agricultural and processed products originating in the poorest associated and non-associated developing countries;
47. Recognises that the concessions made during the Tokyo Round in respect of agricultural products and processed agricultural products from the developing countries are inadequate; considers that the generalised system of preferences applicable after 1980 should be improved as regards both
- the quantities and types of products which benefit from the tariff concessions, and
- the simplicity, effectiveness and flexibility of its operation, so as to take particular account of the requirements of the poorest developing countries which have hitherto derived insufficient benefit from the system;
48. Considers that the Community should actively help to stabilise and improve the organisation of the major international markets, in particular the agricultural markets;
49. Calls on the Commission and Council
(a) to take steps to ensure the early and effective operation of the 'Common Fund for the Stabilisation of Commodity Markets' and the implementation of the 'Integrated Programme for Raw Materials';
(b) to encourage, as regards the various agricultural and mineral products, the conclusion of agreements designed to stabilise prices in accordance with the Unctad guidelines, and in particular by the building up of buffer stocks;
50. Calls on the Commission and Council to contribute actively by suitable measures, to the stabilisation of the export revenue of the developing countries;
51. Calls for the Community to join the International Sugar Agreement, in accordance with the declaration made at the last meeting of the EEC-ACP Joint Committee in Arusha;
52. Requests the Community to take an active part in the preparations for the resumption of the negotiations on a new international cereals agreement, which should be regarded as the keystone of the new international food order (and which should be concluded by mid-1981), and to make every effort to ensure that this agreement provides a satisfactory solution for the establishment of emergency stocks in the developing countries;
53. Considers that there is an urgent need for international rules governing the activities of multinational companies in order, on the one hand, to eliminate their adverse effects and to bring them into line with the development needs of the developing countries and, on the other hand, to provide a reliable reference for private and public investment; requests the governments of the Member States to give explicit instructions to their representatives so that the work in progress at the United Nations and in its agencies may soon produce concrete results; feels also that, as an initial step, it would be useful for the Community to draw up, as soon as possible, its own code of conduct for multinationals taking the Treaty as its starting-point;
54. Requests the Commission and Council to encourage, through appropriate financial and technical cooperation instruments, the economic independence of developing countries, in particular by contribution to the creation of the

developing countries' own economic structures for production, processing and marketing;

55. Takes the view that the Community should support any initiative (for example, economic and regional groupings of developing countries) designed to strengthen the developing countries' negotiating capacity and their collective autonomy;

56. Instructs the Committee on Development and Cooperation, together with the other competent committees, to

(a) monitor progress in the implementation of the guidelines and proposals contained in this resolution, as regards
   - the decisions which must be taken at Community level,
   - the measures which must be taken either by individual Member States or collectively in political cooperation,
   - Community initiatives in the context of major international negotiations;

(b) submit to it a regular report on the food situation and the results achieved in the campaign against hunger and malnutrition, with particular reference to the Community's contribution;

57. Instructs its President to forward this resolution to the Council and Commission, and to the Secretary-General of the UNO and to its specialised agencies.

Joint Declaration by EEC and ACP on the Accession of Greece to the EEC

THE CONTRACTING PARTIES

Considering that the enlargement process of the EEC can be a cause of concern to the ACP States, the EEC's main preferential partners;

Considering therefore that all the means provided for in the Lomé Convention must be implemented in order to settle, in the usual spirit of cooperation between the EEC and the ACP States, the problems which may arise consequent upon the accession of Greece or of future accessions to the Community.

HAVE AGREED AS FOLLOWS:

1. Within the framework of any acceleration of the timetable for the reduction of customs duties and charges having equivalent effect that the Hellenic Republic might decide upon in accordance with the Act of Accession, for the products listed in Annex I, the Hellenic Republic undertakes to apply the same reductions vis à vis the ACP States, and shall endeavour to give priority to certain products which are of special interest to the ACP States.
2. With regard to the preferential treatment applied by some ACP States in respect of imports of products originating in the Community, the Contracting Parties shall consult on the conditions of implementation of article 9(2) (a) of the Convention in respect of the Hellenic Republic during the transitional period provided for by the Protocol with a view to finding mutually acceptable solutions. These consultations shall take place before the 1st January 1982.
3. During the negotiations for the Protocol the ACP States informed the Community of their concern over the accession of Greece. The Community, nothing this concern, confirms to the ACP States that all the procedures for information and consultation provided for in the Lomé Convention shall be fully and immediately put into practice should the application of the protocol cause difficulties for the ACP States in matters of trade cooperation, with a view to seeking mutually acceptable solutions.
4. Understanding the concern expressed by the ACP States over the negotiations for the accession of Spain and Portugal, the Community shall, within the framework of consultation procedures provided for by the Convention, keep the ACP States appropriately informed of developments in these negotiations and shall proceed in good time to any necessary discussion of the possible effects for the ACP States of the enlargement of the Community. In accordance with the provisions of Article 181 of the Lomé Convention, the Community and the ACP States shall take, as necessary, the appropriate measures of adaptation and transition.

Verbal communication from Mr Pisani (Brussels, 2 July 1981)

1. By decision of 4 August 1980 the Council and the representatives of the ECSC Member States' Governments meeting in Council authorised the Commission to open negotiations with the ACP States for the purpose of determining the adjustments and transitional measures necessitated by the accession of Greece.

The negotiations with the ACP States have now been completed and the chairman of the two delegations on 24 June initialled the draft protocols to the second Lomé ACP-EEC Convention concluded by the EEC and the ECSC Member States with the ACP States.

2. The protocols are consonant with what has already been done vis-à-vis many other preferential countries, and were moreover endorsed by the ACP Ambassadors and the Member States' Permanent Representatives at the meeting of the ACP-EEC Committee of Ambassadors on 19 June.

It is urgently necessary that they should be signed in order that the ratification procedures may be begun as soon as possible, in accordance with the ACP-EEC Council of Ministers' decision on 10 April.

3. I propose that the Commission recommend the Council and the Member States to sign them without delay.

Formal Procedure for Approving Non-Associate Aid

Council Regulation (EEC) No 442/81

of 17 February 1981 on financial and technical aid to non-associated developing countries

THE COUNCIL OF THE EUROPEAN COMMUNITIES.

Having regard to the Treaty establishing the European Economic Community, and in particular Article 235 thereof,

Having regard to the proposal from the commission (1),

Having regard to the opinion of the European Parliament (2),

Whereas the pursuit of a Community development cooperation policy calls for *inter alia* the carrying out of certain financial and technical aid operations for the benefit of non-associated developing countries, taking account of the economic principles and priorities established by those countries and having regard to the aspirations of the developing countries towards promoting their development on the basis of their own efforts and of the resources available to them;

Whereas the implementation of such operations would be likely to contribute to the attainment of the Community's objectives;

Whereas the Council, in a resolution of 16 July 1974, confirmed the principle of Community financial and technical aid to non-associated developing countries;

Whereas the action to be taken to implement such aid, the objectives to be attained and the detailed rules of administration should be laid down;

Whereas provision should be made for a procedure involving the participation of a committee composed of representatives of the Member States;

Whereas the Treaty does not provide the specific powers of action for this purpose,

HAS ADOPTED THIS REGULATION:

Article 1

The Community shall implement measures for financial and technical aid to non-associated developing countries on the basis of the criteria provided for in this Regulation.

---

(1) OJ No C 54, 4. 3. 1977, p. 5.

(2) OJ No C 118, 16. 5. 1977, p. 60.

Article 2

The aid shall be directed as a general rule towards the poorest developing countries.

Bearing this principle in mind, a Community presence should be ensured in the major regions of the developing world while aiming at a reasonable geographical balance among these regions.

Article 3

1. The aid shall be mainly directed towards improving the living conditions of the most needy sections of the population of the countries concerned.
2. Special importance shall be attached to the development of the rural environment and to improving food production.

As a subsidiary form of action, participation in regional projects may be considered.

3. Part of the aid shall be earmarked for measures to deal with exceptional circumstances, in particular projects to promote reconstruction in the event of disasters, where such projects are not financed from other Community funds.

Any unallocated, part of the reserve in question shall be released on 31 October of each year to be allocated in some other way, on a proposal from the Commission, in accordance with the procedure laid down in Article 14.

Article 4

Aid shall be granted by the Community either autonomously or, for a substantial share, by means of co-financing with Member States or with multilateral or regional bodies. Wherever possible, the Community nature of the aid shall be maintained.

Article 5

Community aid shall, as a general rule, be in the form of grants.

Article 6

1. Aid may cover expenditure on imports and local expenditure required to carry out projects and programmes.

Taxes, duties and charges and the purchase price of land shall be excluded from Community financing.

2. Maintenance and operating expenses for training and research programmes and for other projects may be covered following a case-by-case examination by the Committee referred to in *Article 11*, subject to the proviso that aid for other projects can only be given at the launching stage and in decreasing amounts.
3. In cases of co-financing, however, due account shall be taken in each case of the relevant procedures applied by the other aid donors.

Article 7

1. For those operations, for which the Community is the sole source of external aid, participation in calls for tenders. invitations to tender, and purchasing and other contracts shall be open on equal terms to all natural or legal persons of Member States and the recipient State.

Such participation may be extended to other developing countries which are recipients of aid under this Regulation during the same financial year or one of the two preceding financial years.
2. Paragraph 1 shall also apply to co-financing operations.
3. However, in cases of co-financing, the participation of third countries in calls for tenders, invitations to tender, and purchasing and other contracts may be allowed only after case-by-case examination by the Committee referred to in *Article 11*.

Article 8

The Commission shall administer the aid in accordance with the procedures laid down in this Regulation.

Article 9

1. The funds required for the measures provided for in this Regulation shall be fixed by the general budget of the European Communities.
Projects and programmes thus financed shall be carried out on a multiannual basis pursuant to the Financial Regulation applicable to the said budget.
2. Acting on a proposal from the Commission and after consulting the European Parliament, the Council shall determine, in good time before the end of the year, the general guidelines to be applied to aid for the following year.

Article 10

The choice of measures to be financed on the basis of this Regulation shall be made having regard to the preferences and wishes expressed by the recipient countries concerned.

Article 11

1. A Committee for aid to non-associated developing countries, hereinafter referred to as 'the Committee', shall be set up at the Commission under the chairmanship of a Commission representative and composed of representatives of the Member States.
2. The secretariat of the Committee shall be provided by the Commission.
3. Any rule of procedure for the Committee not laid down in this Regulation shall be decided on by the Council, acting unanimously on a proposal from the Commission.

Article 12

1. The Committee shall deliver an opinion on the draft financing Decisions submitted to it by the Commission.
2. The draft financing Decisions shall be accompanied by a memorandum, the main purpose of which shall be to asses their effectiveness as far as possible by means of an economic and social evaluation relating the results expected from their implementation to the resources to be invested in them.

Article 13

Within one month the Committee shall decide by a qualified majority as laid down in the first indent of Article 148(2) of the Treaty.

Article 14

1. The draft financing Decisions accompanied by the Committee's opinion, or, in the absence of such an opinion, by the result of the vote of the Committee shall be submitted to the Commission.
2. If the Committee's opinion is favourable, the Commission shall take decisions which shall be immediately applicable.
3. In the absence of any favourable opinion of the Committee, the Commission may refer the matter to the Council.

If the Commission refers the matter to the Council, the latter, acting by a qualified majoirty, shall decide at the second meeting following such referral and at the latest within a period of two months.

If the Council approves the draft financing Decision, the Commission shall take decisions which shall be immediately applicable.

If, after its discussions, the Council has not decided by a qualified majority within a period of two months, the Commission may submit a new draft financing Decision to the Committee and shall inform the European Parliament thereof.

Article 15

Once a year the Commission shall, within the framework of the annual review which will be carried out by the Council in accordance with *Article 9*, provide the European Parliament and the Council with information on the administration of Community financial and technical aid to non-associated developing countries.

Article 16

This Regulation shall enter into force on the third day following its publication in the *Official Journal of the European Communities*.

This Regulation shall be binding in its entirety and directly applicable in all Member States.

Done at Brussels, 17 February 1981.

For the Council
The President
D. F. van der MEI

Extracts from the Communiqué of the Ottawa Western Economic Summit July 1981

Relations with developing countries

9. We support the stability, independence and genuine non-alignment of developing countries and reaffirm our commitment to cooperate with them in a spirit of mutual interest, respect and benefit, recognising the reality of our interdependence.

10. It is in our interest, as well as in theirs, that the developing countries should grow and flourish and play a full part in the international economic system commensurate with their capabilities and responsibilities and become more closely integrated in it.

11. We look forward to constructive and substantive discussions with them, and believe the Cancun Summit offers an early opportunity to address our common problems anew.

12. We reaffirm our willingness to explore all avenues of consultation and cooperation with developing countries in whatever forums may be appropriate. We are ready to participate in preparations for a mutually acceptable process of global negotiations in circumstances offering the prospect of meaningful progress.

13. While growth has been strong in most middle-income developing countries, we are deeply conscious of the serious economic problems in many developing countries, and the grim poverty faced especially by the poorer among them. We remain ready to support the developing countries in the efforts they make to promote their economic and social development within the framework of their own social values and traditions. These efforts are vital to their success.

14. We are committed to maintaining substantial and, in many cases, growing levels of official development assistance and will seek to increase public understanding of its importance. We will direct the major portion of our aid to poorer countries, and will participate actively in the United Nations conference on the least developed countries.

15. We point out that the strengthening of our own economies, increasing access to our markets, and removing impediments to capital flows contribute larger amounts of needed resources and technology and thereby complement official aid. The flow of private capital will be further encouraged in so far as the

developing countries themselves provide assurance for the protection and security of investments.

16. The Soviet Union and its partners, whose contributions are meagre, should make more development assistance available, and take a greater share of exports from developing countries, while respecting their independence and non-alignment.

17. We will maintain a strong commitment to the international financial institutions and work to ensure that they have, and use effectively, the financial resources for their important responsibilities.

18. We attach high priority to the resolution of the problems created for the non-oil developing countries by the damaging effects on them of the high cost of energy imports following the two oil price shocks. We call on the surplus oil-exporting countries to broaden their valuable efforts to finance development in non-oil developing countries, especially in the field of energy. We stand ready to cooperate with them for this purpose and to explore with them, in a spirit of partnership, possible mechanisms, such as those being examined in the World Bank, which would take due account of the importance of their financial contributions.

19. We recognise the importance of accelerated food production in the developing world and of greater world food security, and the need for developing countries to pursue sound agricultural and food policies. We will examine ways to make increased resources available for these purposes. We note that the Italian Government has in mind to discuss within the European Community proposals to be put forward in close cooperation with the specialised United Nations institutions located in Rome for special action in this field primarily directed to the poorest countries.

20. We are deeply concerned about the implications of world population growth. Many developing countries are taking action to deal with that problem, in ways sensitive to human values and dignity, and to develop human resources, including technical and managerial capabilities. We recognise the importance of these issues and will place greater emphasis on international efforts in these areas.

21. We reaffirm our strong commitment to maintaining liberal trade policies and to the effective operation of an open multilateral trading system as embodied in the GATT.

22. We will work together to strengthen this system in the interest of all trading countries, recognising that this will involve structural adaptation to changes in the world economy.

23. We will implement the agreements reached in the multilateral trade negotiations and invite other countries, particularly developing countries, to join in these mutually beneficial trading arrangements.

24. We will continue to resist protectionist pressure, since we recognise that any protectionist measure, whether in the form of overt or hidden trade restrictions or in the form of subsidies to prop up declining industries, not only undermines the dynamism of our economies but also, over time, aggravates inflation and unemployment.

25. We welcome the new initiative represented by the proposal of the Consultative Group of eighteen that the GATT contracting parties convene a meeting at ministerial level during 1982, as well as that of the OECD countries in their programme of study to examine trade issues.

26. We will keep under close review the role played by our countries in the smooth functioning of the multilateral trading system with a view to ensuring maximum openness of our markets in a spirit of reciprocity, while allowing for the safeguard measures provided for in the GATT.
27. We endorse efforts to reach agreement by the end of this year on reducing subsidy elements in official export credit schemes.
28. We are confident that, with perseverance, the energy goals we set at Venice for the decade can be achieved, enabling us to break the link between economic growth and oil consumption through structural change in our energy economies.

Select Bibliography of Recent Publications on EEC-Third World Relations

Belgium and Luxembourg

Banque Européene d'Investissement
Modalités de financement dans le cadre de la deuxième convention de Lomé, 1980.
Bouvier, Paule
L'Europe et la coopération au développement, un bilan: la convention de Lomé, Edition de l'Université de Bruxelles, 1980.
Commission of the European Communities
The European Community and ASEAN, Europe Information: External Relations, 2/78, April 1978 and 16/79, February 1979.
– *The European Community and the developing countries*, European Documentation – Periodical 1977/1.
– *Europe-Third World Interdependence: Facts and Figures*, by Michael Noelke, Dossiers: Development Series 2, 1979. (EC/C/24, SER 2).
– *Community-Third World: the Challenge of Interdependence*, by Hager, W. and Noelke, M., Collection Documentation Bulletin: special edition, 1980.
– *Die Zusammenarbeit im Energiebereich mit den Entwicklungsländern und die Rolle der Gemeinschaft*, Bericht der Kommission an den Rat. 1980.

France

Baron, Frederic et Vernier, G.
Le Fonds Européen de développement, PUF, Paris, 1981.
Cheysson, Claude
'Une nouvelle approche de la coopération', *Etudes et Expansion*, Avril-Juin 1979.
Gautron, J.Cl.
'Aide au Tiers-Monde: la CEE donne l'exemple', *Libre-service actualité*, 7 Novembre 1980.
Grjebine, Andre
La nouvelle économie internationale, PUF, Paris, 1981.
Hubert, Agnes
'Europe-Tiers-Monde: vers un deuxiéme élargissement', *Revue du Marché Commun*, Août-Septembre 1980.

Nitsch, Nicolas
'La Communauté Européenne et le Tiers-Monde', *Objectif Europe*, Septembre 1979.
Nitsch, Nicolas
'Lomé II', *France-Eurafrique*, Décembre 1979.
Pisani, Edgard
Défi du monde, campagne d'Europe, Editions Ramsay, Paris, France.
Pisani, Edgard
'Les rencontres ACP/CEE – Marseille 80: un carrefour économique pour 560 millions d'hommes', *Afrique-Industrie Infrastructures/1*, 15 Août 1980.
Ramadier, Paul
'Europe-Tiers-Monde: pour une nouvelle politique de coopération', *La Revue Nouvelle*, Mars 1981.

Germany

Böttcher, Detlev
Entwicklung durch Integration. Das Verhältnis der Europäoschen Gemeinschaft zu Schwarzafrika, Berlin, (Diss.) 1976.
Hansen, Gerda
Die Bezichungen der Staaten des Vorderen Orients zur Europäischen Gemeinschaft. Eine Auswahlbibliographie, Deutsche Orient-Institut, Hamburg, 1979.
Hatem, Samy Afify
The possibilities of economic cooperation and integration between the European Community and the Arab League, Munich, 1981.
Hatem, Samy A. and Tardait, Gilan
Europäisch-Arabischer Dialog, Kiel, 1978.
Institut für Europäische Politik
Europa und die arabische Welt. Probleme und Perspektiven europäischer Arabienpolitik, Europa Union, Bonn, 1975.
Kasenplfug, Hajo
Europäische Gemeinschaft und Dritte Welt, Verl. Weltarchiv, Hamburg, 1975.
Lerche, Dietrich
Grundlagen und Perspektiven des Euro-Arabischen Dialogs, Deutsches Institut für Entwicklungspolitik, Berlin, 1977.
Radermacher, Reiner
Aktuelle Probleme der Beziehungen EG – Lateinamerika aus der Sicht der lateinamerikanischen Staaten, Institut für Iberoamerika-Kunde, Hamburg, 1979.
Regul, Rudolf
Die Europäischen Gemeinschaft und die Mittlemeerländer, Nomos, Baden-Baden, 1977.
Roon, Ger van
Europa und die Dritte Welt. Die Gesichte ihrer Bezieschungen von Beginn der Kolonialseit bis zur Gegenwart, Beck, Munich, 1978.
Schulz, Manfred
Europäische Gemeinschaft und Entiwcklungsländer. Die ungleichen Partner, Diesterweg, Frankfurt a.M., Berlin, Munich, 1978.

Ireland

Matthews, Alan
'The European Community's external trade policy: implications for Ireland', Irish Council of the European Movement, Dublin, 1980.
McAleese, Dermot, and Carey, Patrick
'Employment coefficients for Irish trade with non-EEC countries: measurements and implications', *Economic and Social Review*, January 1981.

Netherlands

Cohen, R.
De tweede ACS-EEG overeenkomst of Lomé II, *Internationale Spectator*, 34:9, 1980.
Faber, G.
Uitbreiding van de Europese Gemeenschap, herstructurering en afhankelijke ontwikkeling, *Maandschrift Economie*, 44:10, 1980.
Faber, G.
De visie van de Nederlandse regering op de EG en ontwikkelings-samenwerking, *Internationale Spectator*, 35:3, 1981.
Jepma, C. J.
Effecten voor de geassocieerden van twintig jaar associatiebeleid van de EEG, *Maandschrift Economie*, 43:2, 1979.
Lanjauw, G. J.
Protectie ten opzichte van ontwikkelingslanden, *Maandschrift Economie*, 45:1, 1981.
Mangé E. A.
Lomé II (EG-Afrika, de Caraiben en de Stille Oceaanlanden), *ESB 65*, 3255, 1980.
Metzemaekers, L.
De 'continuing story' van de Euro-Arabische betrekkingen, *Nieuw Europa*, 6:2, 1980.
Pijpers, A.
De paradoxale ontwikkeling van de Europese buitenlandse politiek, *Internationale Spectator*, 34:7, 1980.
Smits, R. J. H.
De investeringsparagraaf in de nieuwe overeenkomst van Lomé, *S.E.W. Tijdschrift voor Europees en Economisch Recht*, 28:12, 1980.
Vervliet, M.
Europa en de Derde Wereld, *Tijdschrift voor Ontwikkelingss-amenwerking*, 5:2, 1980.
Visser, J. D.
De EEG en de Andesgroep, *Nieuw Europa*, 6:4, 1980.
Wellens, K.
Enkele kanttekeningen bij titel IV (investeringen) van de Tweede Conventie van Lomé, Nederlands Juristenblad, 56:4, 1981.

Scandinavia

EF og tropisk Afrika. Special Issue. *Den Ny Verden*, 13:4, 1979.
Hoffmeyer, Birgit
The EEC and agriculture in the developing countries. Trends in EEC agricultural policy: Possible consequences for the developing countries, Centre for Development Research, Copenhagen, 1981.
Janczewski, Zbigniew
The convention of Lomé, Swedish International Development Authority, Stockholm, 1979.
Raikes, Philip
A select bibliography with comments on the EEC and agriculture in the Third World, Centre for Development Research, Copenhagen, 1980.

United Kingdom

Debatisse, Michel Louis
EEC organisation of the cereals market: principles and consequences, Occasional Paper 10, Centre for European Agricultural Studies, Wye College, Ashford, Kent, 1981.
House of Lords, Select Committee on the European Communities.
Development Aid Policy with Minutes of Evidence, HMSO, London, April 1981.
House of Lords, Select Committee on the European Communities.
Imports of Cereal Substitutes for Use as Animal Feedingstuffs, HMSO, London, July 1981.
Josling, Tim
'The European Community Agricultural Policies and the Interest of Developing Countries', *ODI Review*, 1, 1979.
Long, Frank (ed.)
The Political Economy of EEC Relations with African, Caribbean and Pacific States: Contributions to the Understanding of the Lomé Convention on North-South Relations, Pergamon, Oxford, 1980.
Marsh, John S. and Swanney, Pamela J.
Agriculture and the European Community, Allen & Unwin, London, 1980.
Shlain, Avi and Iannopoulos, G. M. (eds.)
The EEC and the Mediterranean Countries, Cambridge University Press, London, 1976.
Talbot, Ross B.
'The European Community's Food Aid Programme – An integration of ideology, strategy, technology and surpluses', *Food Policy*, 4:4, November 1979.
Twitchett, Carol Cosgrove
A Framework for Development: The EEC and the ACP, Allen & Unwin, London, 1981.
Twitchett, K. J. (ed.)
Europe and the World. The External Relations of the Common Market, Europa Publications, London, 1976.

Index

EEC and the Third World: A Survey 1

A Survey 1 aims to pull together the many strands of EEC (and where relevant member state) policies and actions that affect the Third World. It brings to this analysis the weight of research being undertaken in European centres and elsewhere. It published at a time when particular interest was generated in the relationship between North and South by the report of the 'Brandt' Commission. It contains extensive statistical and documentary appendices as a permanent reference source.

ISBN 0 340 26502 7   160 pp.   235 × 155 mm.   1981.
Paperback   £5.00 net b